SMUTS
A Reappraisal

SMUTS
A Reappraisal

Bernard Friedman

ST. MARTIN'S PRESS NEW YORK

For information, write:
St. Martin's Press, Inc., 175 Fifth Avenue, New York, N.Y. 10010
Library of Congress Catalog Card Number: 75-21835
First published in the United States of America in 1976

Printed in Great Britain

Preface

This is not a biography of Smuts. That work has been accomplished by other hands, notably by Sarah Gertrude Millin, in whose two volumes almost every line is a eulogy, and by W. K. Hancock, whose biography, although less adulatory, presents a portrait with few shadows. They both sustain the legend of Smuts as the great Commonwealth statesman whose commanding stature in world affairs gave South Africa the prestige, if not the status, of a great power.

The present work, an essay in reappraisal, is concerned with his role in the South African scene. It falls into three sections.

The first section tells how he rose to a position of power which enabled him to play a leading part in the making of the Union of South Africa, and how the National Convention, chiefly by his contriving, decided in favour of a unitary and flexible constitution. It concludes with a brief account of the unfortunate consequences which flowed from the adoption of such a constitution.

The second section deals with Smuts's reconciliation with General Hertzog which led to the formation of the 'Fusion Government', generally regarded as the most beneficent Government in the history of South Africa. It recounts the circumstances – initially not beyond his control – which forced him to accept a subordinate and submissive role to General Hertzog and thus to accept responsibility for the retrograde legislation which had the effect of dismantling the last remnants of the Cape liberal tradition; and it describes how, after experiencing further humiliations, he was rescued from an unhappy situation by the advent of World War II.

The third section shows that Smuts, who emerged from the war with his power and prestige immensely enhanced, failed to meet the challenge of the post-war epoch, and that, having no clear and compelling vision of the future, he was unable to provide the dynamic leadership which would have made his party an effective instrument of social change. It shows, further, that both as a politician, concerned with the strategy by which power is gained or retained, and as a statesman, concerned with the ends for which power is used, his record is one of failure, and how his failure paved the way for the triumph of the reactionary forces who now rule South Africa.

Thus, each section, virtually an essay in itself, is concerned with Smuts's role in a clearly defined period, and because the writer has attempted not a biography but a reappraisal, he has chosen for scrutiny the periods which he believes to be the most significant in the career of Smuts as a politician and statesman.

Contents

Section One

The Father of the Constitution

'Amongst the many men who worked together to make the Union of South Africa Smuts was pre-eminent. From start to finish it was his strategy and tactics that dominated the campaign.'

W. K. Hancock, *Smuts*, Vol. I, p. 246

I

The National Convention met in October 1908. Among the statesmen who were gathered together in that historic assembly to prepare a constitution for the Union of South Africa, one of the most eminent was Jan Christiaan Smuts.

His career had prospered ever since his student days at Cambridge. At the University he applied himself to his studies with Miltonic zeal – he scorned delights and lived laborious days. He was the first student ever to attempt both parts of the Law Tripos in one year and was placed first in the examinations. He won the George Long Prize in Roman Law and Jurisprudence, a prize which was awarded only to candidates of the highest distinction and which was seldom awarded because the required standard was seldom attained.

On his return to South Africa, Smuts settled in Johannesburg shortly after the Jameson Raid. He soon caught the perceptive eye of President Kruger and, at the age of 28, was appointed State Attorney of the Transvaal. His relations with the old President were cordial – 'like father and son' said Smuts. And President Kruger described Smuts as 'a man of iron will destined to play a great role in the history of South Africa'. Smuts soon established himself as the most important figure, under the President, in the Transvaal Government. He played a leading part in the negotiations with the British Government, working earnestly for peace and the prevention of war. At a fateful meeting with the British Agent in Pretoria in August 1899, Smuts seemed to be conceding everything that Chamberlain had asked for – a five-year retrospective franchise for the Uitlanders and a quarter of the seats in the Transvaal Parliament, the *Volksraad*. All he asked in return was that Chamberlain should renounce the British claim to suzerainty over the Transvaal. It was Chamberlain's intransigence on this vital issue of suzerainty that convinced Smuts that his exertions were in vain and that war was inevitable.

When war broke out, Smuts led a Boer commando, some 360 strong, in a prolonged guerilla expedition into the Cape Colony with the twofold object of raising a rebellion against the British flag and harassing the long British lines of communication to the main theatre of operations. It was a gallant and hazardous enterprise, daring in conception but meagre in results – save that it enabled Smuts to take his place beside Botha, de la Rey and de Wet as one of the legendary Boer War generals.

Smuts was recalled from his incursion into the Cape Colony to take part in the peace discussions which were in progress at Vereeniging. He was in favour of coming to terms with the British. Like Botha, the Commandant-General of the Boer forces, Smuts had come to the conclusion that nothing but further misery was to be gained by continuing the struggle to the bitter end. He worked closely with Botha to secure as favourable terms as possible from the British, and their joint endeavours at Vereeniging laid the foundation of a remarkable and enduring friendship which was to have a decisive influence on the course of history.

Smuts soon made his presence felt at the Peace Conference. At a crucial moment, when the negotiations ran into difficulties and appeared to have reached an impasse, Kitchener drew Smuts out of the conference chamber. As they paced the stoep[1] together, Kitchener confided to Smuts his conviction that in two years' time a Liberal Government would be in power in England. From a Liberal Government the Boers could expect far more generous treatment than he, Kitchener, was empowered to concede. 'If a Liberal Government comes into power', said Kitchener, 'it will grant you a constitution for South Africa.'

It is surprising to learn that Kitchener, whose rigidity was monumental, was capable of such a subtle piece of diplomacy. The explanation was that Kitchener was anxious to be quit of the whole business of peace-making as a glittering prize awaited him – the office of Commander-in-Chief of the forces in India.

However, the deft manoeuvre worked. Kitchener made it clear that what he had said represented only his own opinion but it was given in good faith. 'That', said Smuts, 'accomplished the peace. We went back and the arrangements at the Conference were definitely concluded and the war came to a close.' [1]

II

When the Liberal Government came into power in 1905 Smuts hurried to London, armed with a lengthy memorandum setting out the case for self-government for the Transvaal. The memorandum was skilfully drafted; every paragraph enshrined some Liberal principle, and the whole document was designed to make a powerful appeal to the Liberal mind. The theme elaborated in the memorandum was clearly stated in its opening paragraphs:

'What South Africa needs above all things after the storms and upheavals of the past is tranquillity. But that can only be secured by the removal of all just grounds of discontent and the unreserved application of Liberal Principles to the government of the new Colonies by securing a statesmanlike trust in the people of the land, of whatever race, and granting them a fair and equitable Constitution under which they can work out their own salvation . . .

'In our opinion the only security for the British connection lies – not in armies and the ostentatious loyalty of mine-owners – but in the trust and goodwill of the people of South Africa as a whole. Let the permanent population (English and Dutch) who are not speculators and birds of passage, come to realise that under the British flag there are peace and contentment, there are justice and equal rights for all, and there is the free scope to follow their own national ideals and destiny. . . . I can conceive no nobler task for Liberal statesmanship than that it may inaugurate in South Africa such an era of trust and goodwill and reliance on the people of the land, and bring healing to the wounds which the errors of the past have inflicted.' [2]

However, his interviews with Lloyd George, Morley, Elgin and the young Winston Churchill gave him little encouragement. Churchill asked him if he knew of a case where a conquered people were allowed to govern themselves and said he was asking too much. Smuts, it seemed, would have to return empty-handed to South Africa; but, fortunately, he succeeded in obtaining a second interview with the Prime Minister, Sir Henry Campbell-Bannerman. Smuts himself has given us an account of this historic interview:

'I put a simple case before him that night in 10 Downing Street. It was in substance: "Do you want friends or enemies? You can have the Boers for friends and they have proved what quality that friendship may mean. I pledge the friendship of my colleagues and myself if you wish it. You can choose to make them enemies, and possibly to have another Ireland on your hands. If you do believe in liberty, it is also their faith and their religion." I used no set arguments, but simply spoke to him as man to man and appealed only to the human aspect, which I felt would weigh deeply with him. He was a cautious Scot and said nothing to me, but yet I left that room that night a happy man. My intuition told me that the thing had been done.' [3]

'That talk', said Smuts, 'settled the future of South Africa.' [4]

At the Cabinet meeting the following morning Campbell-Bannerman, in a speech which Lloyd George described as the finest he had ever heard and which reduced one Minister to tears, persuaded his colleagues to accept a policy of trust and magnanimity towards the conquered Boers and grant them the measure of self-government they asked for. But are we to believe that Campbell-Bannerman's eloquent appeal to his colleagues was the result of a sudden and dramatic conversion by Smuts? Such an interpretation gives too little credit to Campbell-Bannerman and too much credit to Smuts. The British Prime Minister gave Smuts a sympathetic hearing because he had already committed himself to the kind of policy – a policy of trust and magnanimity – which Smuts had urged upon him.

As far back as 1901, while the Boer war was still being fought, Campbell-Bannerman had declared: 'If we are to maintain the political supremacy of the British power in South Africa it can only be by conciliation and friendship: it will never be by domination and ascendancy unless it rests upon the willing consent of a sympathetic and contented people.' [5] And a year before his advent to power Campbell-Bannerman had publicly committed himself to the granting of self-government to the Boers, under the British Crown. What troubled him now was in essence a question of timing. Only four years had elapsed since the Boers had laid down their arms. Was the time ripe for an act of trust and magnanimity? Would the generous act of giving ex-enemies their freedom be enough to ensure their allegiance? What, if after a century of Anglo-Afrikaner antagonism culminating in a recent and bitter war, the Boers remained sullen and irreconcilable? To subdue the rebellious Boers and restore the Imperial authority, the British would be compelled to fight the Boer War all over again, otherwise the policy of trust would prove to be no more than a policy of surrender. Did this mean in effect that a liberal solution was just not feasible in existing circumstances?

It was Smuts who dispelled Campbell-Bannerman's fears and, at the momentous interview, convinced him that it was not too soon to implement the policy to which he was so deeply committed both by his liberal professions and his pledged word. It would be ungracious therefore to deny Smuts his meed of glory for a praiseworthy achievement. This historic episode glowed in his memory ever afterwards and he always regarded his successful interview with Campbell-Bannerman as one of the greatest achievements of his life. For Campbell-Bannerman, Smuts retained the highest regard; he could pay that Liberal statesman no greater tribute than to compare him with Botha, ranking them as men of equal stature. And how indeed could Smuts fail to recognise greatness in a statesman who had proved responsive to a poignant plea on behalf of a gallant and dispossessed people?

III

In the elections which followed the grant of self-government, *Het Volk*,[2] the party led by Botha with Smuts as his second-in-command, gained a substantial majority over all other parties. Accordingly Botha became Prime Minister and Smuts was given the key post of Colonial Secretary and was also appointed Minister of Mines. Botha and Smuts were a formidable combination. Botha reigned and Smuts ruled. Botha was the father-figure, an important role in the Boer patriarchal society. Botha had a charisma compounded of a homespun wisdom, innate chivalry and personal magnetism; he was as much respected by his British conquerors as he was revered by the Boer veterans whom he had commanded in the field. To the rugged, sturdy Boers he was readily accessible; they brought their problems and petitions to him, just as in the days before the war they had brought them to Kruger, who used to receive them on the broad stoep where the dour and dignified old President held court. Smuts, a Cassius-like figure beside the burly Louis Botha, was content to live in the shadow of his political chief, although greatly his intellectual superior. The relationship between them was close and congenial; in the conduct of affairs, the graciousness of Botha was matched by the generosity of Smuts, for Botha allowed Smuts to do all the work and Smuts allowed Botha to enjoy all the prestige. In the cabinet of six, Smuts was undoubtedly the dynamic force; with the commanding figure of Botha beside him, Smuts was definitely in the driver's seat, the reins of government firmly in his grasp.

The grant of self-government – Britain's act of magnanimity – was followed by a remission of a war debt of £3,000,000 together with a loan of £5,000,000 to repair the ravages of war. The wounds of war, however, were deep and slow to heal. Memories of the recent conflict were still bitter – they hurt and rankled. Botha and Smuts saw clearly that only a healing process involving all sections of the community could redress the grievances of the past and restore peace and tranquillity in the future. Accordingly, they decided upon a policy of conciliation. (The word 'reconciliation' would probably have defined their aim more precisely.) In essence the policy of conciliation was a call to forgive and forget so that Briton and Boer should be drawn together in a common love for their country and face the tasks of the future in a spirit of mutual trust. The policy of conciliation was basically a response to the magnanimity of the British Government in granting self-rule to the former republics so soon after the war. It was not only an act of magnanimity: it was also a great act of faith.

Five years after the Peace of Vereeniging, which ended the two Boer Republics, these selfsame territories were ruled under the British crown by the defeated Boer generals who had signed the terms of surrender. The fate of the English-speaking section was in the hands of their former enemies! Botha and Smuts were constantly mindful of this responsibility – they regarded it as an obligation of honour to ensure that the English-speaking section should have no occasion to regret or suffer for this great act of faith. The policy of conciliation was a fine piece of statesmanship with more than a touch of the nobility of vision which inspired Abraham Lincoln to rise above the passions of war 'with charity for all and malice towards none'. Moreover, the policy of conciliation could be extended beyond the borders of the Transvaal and find its logical consummation in a federation or union of the four British colonies. Indeed in the memorandum to the British Government which he had carried with him to London, Smuts predicted with confidence that 'the question of federation or perhaps even unification will become a practical one as soon as responsible government has been granted to the new colonies . . . with a truly popular constitution in the Transvaal we may see federation or union within the next five years'.

The policy of conciliation was not only morally unassailable, it was also politically rewarding. In the Transvaal the voting strength of the English-speaking section was somewhat greater than that of the Afrikaans-speaking section. In his own constituency, for example, Smuts had to gain the support of a fair proportion of English-speaking voters to win or retain his seat. Botha and Smuts were therefore doubly committed to a policy of conciliation which had the two-fold merit of being sound in principle and prudent in practice – for a politician a rare but happy conjuncture.

IV

The policy of conciliation was designed to ensure a tranquil and prosperous future for Briton and Boer in a regenerated South Africa. But what of the Native?[3] What provision was there for him in the new scheme of things? In Smuts's famous memorandum there was no trace of concern for the fate of the Black man. It was a glaring omission. Merriman, to whom Smuts had confided a copy of his memorandum prior to his departure for London, was quick to observe the absence of any reference to the Native question. He wrote to Smuts:

'What struck me at once in reading your admirable remarks on liberal principles was that they were open to the same objection in kind as the American Declaration of Independence, viz. that you ignore three-quarters of the population because they are coloured . . . I do not like the Natives at all and I wish we had no Black man in South Africa. But there they are, our lot is cast with them by an overruling Providence and the only question is how to shape our course so as to maintain the supremacy of our race and at the same time do our duty. Two courses are open. One is the Cape policy of recognising the right to the franchise irrespective of colour of all who qualify . . . The second method which is that adopted by the two Republics and Natal, viz. the total disfranchisement of the Native. What promise of permanency does this plan give? What hope for the future does it hold out? These people are numerous and increasing both in wealth and numbers . . . They are the workers and history tells us that the future is to the workers.' [6]

In reply to Merriman, Smuts wrote:

'With much that you say I most cordially agree, . . . I sympathise profoundly with the Native races of South Africa whose land it was long before we came here to force a policy of dispossession on them . . . But I don't believe in politics for them. Perhaps at bottom I do not believe in politics at all as a means for the attainment of the highest ends, but certainly so far as the Natives are concerned politics will to my mind only have an unsettling influence. I would therefore not give them the franchise, which in any case would not affect more than a negligible number of them at present. When I consider the political future of the Natives in South Africa I must say that I look into shadows and darkness; and then I feel inclined to shift the intolerable burden of solving the sphinx problem to the ampler shoulders and stronger brains of the future.' [7]

Smuts's reply is important because it was an early manifestation of what was to be a life-long attitude to the Native question. Liberal principles, it seems, could be successfully invoked in the case of the Boers, but they somehow lost their efficacy where the Natives were concerned. In principle liberalism is a fine doctrine, but in practice it is for Whites only. The Natives, according to Smuts, must look to means other than politics for the attainment of the highest ends. But freedom surely is one of the highest ends. By what mysterious means other than politics is freedom attainable? And if freedom, as one of the highest ends, is attainable by means other than politics, why did Smuts dedicate himself to the use of inferior means? On the other hand, if the other and more exalted means of attaining freedom are not accessible to the Natives why should they be denied the use of politics which Smuts was using so successfully to gain freedom for the Boers?

The truth of the matter is that his famous memorandum, firmly grounded in liberal doctrine, was designed to reflect the political philosophy of the Government to which it was addressed; it did not represent Smuts's own credo. If he had accepted liberalism as his creed, it would have provided him with sufficient light to penetrate the darkness to which he so readily surrendered; he would have seen his way ahead at least as clearly as Merriman was able to discern it. In his attitude to the Natives Smuts was not wanting in benevolence; he sincerely desired their advancement but his concern for them was paternal. In this respect Smuts was a true Afrikaner – paternalism was a tradition which he was always ready to honour. Politically, his concern for the Natives advanced no further than the concept of Guardianship. (The term 'Trusteeship' came into use much later.) Guardianship exercised its authority on the assumption that the Natives were still at a primitive stage of development and must be treated as wards. Guardianship may have satisfied the Calvinist conscience of the Afrikaner, but it was no more than a plausible substitute for a policy. It was in itself not a policy because it raised more questions than it could answer. Has guardianship not a duty to ensure the progress of the wards to maturity? If guardianship recognises no such obligation, will it not tend to become a permanent institution, more concerned with maintaining the privileged status of the guardian than advancing the interests of the wards, and thus prove to be no more than a cloak for White supremacy? And even if the guardian displays no excess of zeal in helping the wards to advance towards maturity, will not their contact with the civilised values which the guardian represents kindle aspirations which, if not satisfied, must lead to a spirit of revolt? Sooner or later the wards will emerge from a state of tutelage: they will be ripe for emancipation. Will they have a say in the making of the laws which govern them? Will they have access to the normal democratic process by which grievances are redressed? Will they have representation in Parliament?

It is because Smuts would offer no clear-cut answers to these questions that he failed to develop a consistent, enlightened and constructive approach to the Native problem.

In the field of public affairs he was the most capable man of his time; if he had set his incisive mind to work on the subject, he could undoubtedly have risen to the conception of Native progress as a great – perhaps the supreme – aim of State policy and could, accordingly, have laid down guidelines to ensure the gradual advance of the Natives towards clearly-defined goals. He played a leading part in public affairs for more than fifty years; he held high office for most of this time, and as Prime Minister he wielded almost dictatorial power; it is melancholy to reflect that during all that period, even during the years of his ascendancy, he made no seminal contribution towards a solution of the Native question. As far as he was concerned, the Native question was not a problem to be solved but an embarrassment to be shelved. In the field of Native affairs he was content to practise a cautious pragmatism, meeting emergent situations with temporising expedients.

This pragmatism exposed him to the charge that he had no Native policy and he experienced the full effect of this indictment in more than one election. He had to face opponents whose cry at the hustings was '*swart gevaar*'[4], who relied on a naked and unbridled appeal to fear and prejudice and who insisted that any concessions to the Kaffirs, even the slightest, would end in complete surrender to Black domination. As he could offer no alternative policy, he had to descend to the level of his opponents; they imposed their strategy upon him and compelled him to contest the issue on terms which, from the very outset, yielded the victory to the forces of obscurantism. To suffer defeat at the hands of such opponents was a bitter and humiliating experience for Smuts. If he had stood for an enlightened Native policy against opponents who owed their success to a crude appeal to colour prejudice, it would at least have saved his defeats from ignominy – it would even have enhanced his claim to statesmanship. Even statesmen of the stature of a Gladstone or a Lincoln had their defeats as well as their victories. But their conduct of affairs was distinguished by a fidelity to high principle. They fought for causes which exalted their victories and redeemed their defeats. Their achievements they left as a legacy to posterity. Their unfinished tasks could be entrusted to the political parties which were committed to their principles and dedicated to their aims. When Smuts died he left his defeated party no legacy save his great name. They continued, of course, to use his name as a rallying-cry but as it was associated with no sustaining vision that could provide their party with an identity and a sense of destiny, it was not enough to make their sojourn in the wilderness a purposeful sojourn and thus ensure their eventual return to power.

This analysis, however, takes us too far into the future. At the beginning of 1908, the year after the successful inauguration of self-government, Smuts turned his attention to the task of bringing about a united South Africa. He had now to concentrate on the task of constitution-making. Should he plan for a federation or a union? Should he think in terms of a constitution which was federal and rigid, or a constitution which was unitary and flexible? It was a question of crucial importance. There was no facile answer; the choice of constitution could not be determined, as if it were an academic exercise, by weighing the abstract merits of the one political system against the abstract merits of the other.

V

The makers of the Union were faced with an almost insoluble problem – their task was to devise a constitution which would succeed in bringing together two entirely different traditions, represented by the Cape on the one hand, and the three northern colonies on the other.

The Cape had a liberal tradition. As far back as 1853, it had received a constitution which established a parliament for the Cape. A historic dispatch from the Duke of Newcastle to the Governor of the Cape, Sir George Cathcart, reveals the spirit in which the constitution was granted:

'It is the earnest desire of Her Majesty's government that

all her subjects at the Cape without distinction of class or colour should be united by one bond of loyalty and we believe that the exercise of political rights enjoyed by all alike will prove one of the best methods of attaining this object.'

The constitution conferred on the Cape of Good Hope was as liberal as any constitution to be found in the British Empire. The franchise was open to all men, White, Coloured or Native, who could comply with a civilisation test and every person qualified to vote was eligible for election to the House of Assembly.

The northern colonies, on the other hand, had a rigid colour bar in their constitutions. In the Transvaal and the Orange River Colony there was an absolute exclusion from the franchise and from public office of every person who was not a European. The northern republics had in fact been founded by the Voortrekkers because they preferred to go into exile rather than accept the egalitarian principles which British rule sought to establish in the Cape. The famous Ordinance of 1828 abolished the offence of vagrancy and abolished passes for the indigenous population, thus establishing the principle of legal equality for all free men. And in 1834 the slaves of the Cape were declared free. The Boer settlers – farmers and frontiersmen – were not prepared to accept equality of status for White and Black. Emotionally and politically they were not conditioned to submit to such a principle. Better to go into exile than live under British rule. And into exile they went.

In 1835 began the great migration northwards known as the 'Great Trek'. Louis Trichardt led the first contingent of farmers and frontiersmen into the unexplored interior and other groups followed. One is still amazed at the courage which took these men and their ox-wagons on their long journey northwards into the legendary lands of the Kaffir. Deeply imbued with the spirit of the Old Testament, the Voortrekkers likened themselves to the Israelites; they were prepared to face the hazards and hardships of the wilderness rather than endure the decrees of the modern Pharaoh. In their search for the new Canaan they inevitably came into conflict with the Black hordes. Bred in the tradition of slavery, reared in the spirit of the frontier, where life was a constant struggle between White and Black for the fertile grasslands which both sides claimed as their own, they were schooled in the harsh doctrine that security for the White man lay in subduing the Black man and keeping him subdued. Accordingly the scattered White communities, living among primitive people, claimed the conqueror's right to rule and keep the Black man in a state of complete subjection. They would admit of no relationship between White and Black save that of master and servant. The caste system they established was supported by Biblical sanction, than which they recognised no higher authority. White supremacy was part of the Divine order of things. Equality of status for White and Black was not only a revolutionary conception – it was sheer blasphemy. No equality in Church or State was the principle upon which their constitutions were founded.

Natal, although it was always a British colony, tended to lean in its attitude to the Native question towards the two former Republics. The White communities in Natal grew up under the shadow of the Zulu Kingdom; the Zulus, a proud warrior people, were a serious threat to the White settlements in and around Durban. As late as 1897 a British force was wiped out without a survivor at the battle of Isandhlwana, during the Zulu war. Durban was therefore much closer to the perils of the frontier than Cape Town, and consequently Natal, although predominantly British, was markedly less liberal than the Cape Colony. In theory the Natal Native could obtain the franchise on the grant of a certificate from the Governor. Such certificates, however, were conceded in only a few cases. In practice therefore the Natal Natives were denied the vote. The Whites of Natal, in their attitude to the Natives, were conscious of a natural superiority which required no Biblical texts to give it a warrant of respectability.

The makers of the Union therefore faced a challenging situation. They could not erase the past. They could not create a blank sheet to write on. There existed objective factors which had to be taken into account. Each of the four colonies had its own history. The colonies had drifted apart; they had engaged in bitter conflict; they had developed their own political systems, which were based on fundamentally different conceptions of human rights. On what basis could these States be reconciled? How could the makers of the constitution bridge the gulf created by the divergence of view between the Cape and the northern colonies on the political status of the Natives in the future Union?

Only one man saw the situation clearly. W. P. Schreiner, a former Prime Minister of the Cape, was deeply concerned about the fate of the non-Whites in the future Union. In his view the Native question, or, as he preferred to call it, the Colour question, was a factor of basic importance in determining the character of the constitution. In a reply to a letter from Smuts, he wrote as follows:

'We must approach the subject [of Union] in a perfectly open and candid manner, and I am bound to respond by saying that to my mind the fundamental question is that of our policy regarding "Colour". I prefer to put it in that form myself – because the "Native question" is a far less precise phrase than the "Colour question".

'*Humani nil a me alienum puto*. To embody in the South African constitution a vertical line or barrier separating its people upon the ground of colour into a privileged class or caste and an unprivileged, inferior proletariat is, as I see the problem, as imprudent as it would be to build a grand building upon unsound and sinking foundations . . . How Union, as you nobly plead its cause is to be reconciled with justice and freedom, is then the great problem. Is there not here to be found perhaps some difference between our standpoint. I hope not.' [8]

Schreiner, one of the great figures in South African history, is not so well known as his famous sister, Olive Schreiner; he shared with her a deep humanism, to which his fine legal mind gave a keen cutting edge. He insisted that a concern for human rights should govern the making of a constitution and should determine its final character. To him the Cape non-racial franchise was of paramount importance. He was justly proud of the fact that in the Cape – the largest and oldest of the colonies – they had a political system which was based on a respect for the worth and dignity of the human person, irrespective of race or colour. In the Cape, in contradistinction to the other colonies, the principle of equality was enshrined in the Constitution. In the social sphere prejudice might still be strong; as in every race-conscious society, the conventional barriers to the social mingling of the races were almost insuperable. But over the wider area where law and not convention prevailed, prejudice was a diminishing factor, and relations between the races were peaceful – even good-humoured – and free from tension. The fulfilment of the liberal dream, if not yet attained, was definitely attainable. For the constitution provided a reliable framework for the growth and development of an open society – a society where every individual could rise to his full stature, where every individual was free to contribute according to his ability and to reap the corresponding reward, where a man's intrinsic worth and not the colour of his skin determined his status and established his claim to the respect of his fellows. To Schreiner, the Cape political system, because of the non-racial franchise which was its heart, constituted a most precious heritage; if the Cape was to enter into some form of Union, it could enter only on terms which would ensure that the non-racial franchise would remain inviolate.

Schreiner was therefore strongly in favour of a federal constitution; only a federal constitution would respect the Cape liberal tradition and safeguard its non-racial franchise. From his point of view the case for such a constitution was unassailable. It has been well said that a federal constitution guarantees to the constituent regions the right to be different; it enables the constituent regions to preserve what is of peculiar value and importance to them. In view of the fact that the Cape differed fundamentally from the other States in respect of its tradition and political institutions, a federal constitution was precisely the safeguard it required. A federal constitution ensures a complete separation of powers as between the central authority and the constituent regions. It confers upon the central authority power over matters of common concern, such as external affairs, defence, customs, currency and immigration; but the central authority is precluded by the constitution from interfering with matters which are the concern of the constituent regions. In a federal system, it is the function of the courts to ensure that the central authority on the one hand and the constituent regions on the other restrict their legislation to their respective areas of competence. A federal constitution, moreover, has the merit of being a rigid constitution; this means that it cannot be altered or amended in any way save by a special procedure designed to ensure general consent. The Constitution of the United States is the classical example of a rigid constitution: it cannot be altered or amended in any respect save by a two-thirds majority of the Senate and House of Representatives, and by a two-thirds majority of three-quarters of the State legislatures. A rigid constitution is the only method by which the effective control of the powers allocated to the constituent regions can be guaranteed to them. It was precisely the kind of constitution Schreiner wanted.

Smuts, however, had decided in favour of a unitary constitution. It was no sudden decision. At one time his mind had wavered between a federal and a unitary system. In July 1907, writing to Merriman, he said, 'You know I am an enthusiast for federation or (if possible) unification,' and in August of the same year he wrote, 'My own position is that federation or rather unification is a good and wise ideal'. It seems clear that he always had a personal bias in favour of a unitary system but was assailed by grave doubts as to whether it was politically feasible. He was himself a 'Kaapenaar'[5]; he was fully conscious of the irreconcilable differences between the Cape and the northern colonies on the fundamental issue of political rights for the Natives. Very important too was the fact that Natal was anxious to preserve its British character and feared that in a complete union it would come under Afrikaner domination. And the Orange River Colony, the smallest of the four colonies in terms of population, was equally anxious to preserve its Afrikaner identity. What, then, made Smuts finally decide in favour of a unitary system?

It seems that Smuts was greatly influenced by Merriman.

From the very first Merriman, whose role in the making of the Union was second only to that of Smuts, was strongly in favour of what he called a 'legislative union'. Merriman, noted for his austerity in matters of public finance, favoured a unitary system chiefly for reasons of economy; he was opposed to a federal system because he believed that South Africa could not afford such an extravagant form of government. Smuts no doubt felt that, having the powerful support of Merriman, the Cape could be induced to accept a complete union; and if the Cape and the Transvaal stood together on this issue, they could overcome the predilection of Natal and the Orange River Colony for a federal system. It is probable, however, that personal ambition played a decisive part in shaping his determination to work for a unitary system. Smuts had a strong appetite for power. He had already established his ascendancy in the Transvaal. A united South Africa, in which the Transvaal would of course play the dominant role, would offer far greater scope for the exercise of his executive authority. To be in control of the central directing levers of a vast and comprehensive legislative and administrative machine – what an enticing dream for an ambitious politician! It is not surprising therefore that he was fired by the vision of one united South Africa under one central authority, exercising its sovereign sway over the whole land from the Cape to the Limpopo.

In the Transvaal Legislature he explained his preference for a unitary and flexible constitution in the following terms:

'. . . To my mind the great difficulty with federation is this, that it assumes that a number of independent parties come together and enter into a compact, into an agreement, which is binding for the future . . . The natural result of that system is that it becomes a hide-bound system . . . and the result is a rigid, inflexible constitution which cannot develop as times go forward. Is that the sort of constitution we want for South Africa, for a country in its infancy? Do we want a constitution which will lead to civil wars as the American Constitution led to? No; we prefer to follow a different type – that of the British Constitution . . .' [9]

And Mrs Millin tells us that Smuts, in planning for Union, studied in particular the American Constitution. 'He decided, however, that the American Constitution was too rigid, gave the federal states too much power and the central authority too little,' she says, and adds 'He envied England indeed, that had no written constitution at all, no document limiting the power of Parliament.' [10]

It is clear that Smuts's case against federation was based on the American experience. The American Constitution, being a federal constitution, was too rigid; it was incapable of being amended. It therefore led to civil war. But was the British Constitution, which Smuts admired because it was so flexible, not open to a similar indictment? The attempt to amend the British Constitution at the time of the Reform Bill plunged the country into a turmoil and brought it to the verge of a revolution, narrowly averted by a timely concession on the part of the British ruling class. And even whilst Smuts was extolling the merits of the British Constitution, Ireland was in the throes of an agitation for Home Rule, a separatist movement which eventually culminated in armed insurrection. The British Constitution was a unifying force for England, Scotland and Wales; it was an intolerable yoke for Ireland.

What is so disconcerting to the constitution-maker, seeking to learn from past experience, is that countries like Britain and even the United States, although in a briefer span, have a surfeit of history – a history so rich and varied that it can yield sufficient evidence either to vindicate or condemn their political systems. The American Constitution which Gladstone eulogised, and which made the United States, in the words of Lincoln, 'the last, the best hope of mankind' was, according to Smuts, open to the indictment that it was conducive to civil war. From the practical point of view it is impossible to decide by the study of precedents whether the best constitution is either unitary or federal in structure. There is no ideal pattern on which a constitution can be constructed. A constitution must be tailor-made to suit the conditions of the country for which it is designed. In South Africa the objective factors clearly argued in favour of a federal system. These factors were ineluctable; they could not be spirited away by some rite of incantation; they had to be taken into account. The American Constitution, which Smuts disliked so strongly, was not the only one of its kind. There were other constitutions, notably those of Canada and Australia – in some respects superior to the American Constitution – which could have served as models, and could even have been improved upon in the process of adapting the federal system to South Africa.

Schreiner's approach to the problem of constitution-making was undoubtedly more realistic than Smuts's. It took full account of the objective factors. Smuts, however, was not prepared to yield to Schreiner's point of view. If he were to concede that Schreiner was right and that the Native question was of paramount importance in deciding the character of the Constitution, it would have shattered his dream of a unitary state. He would have had to accept Schreiner's view that only a federal system could safeguard the political status of the Natives in the Cape. Smuts was an adroit politician in the sense that he was always capable of a skilful manoeuvre to secure his own position. If the objective factors could not be overcome, then the area of debate must be narrowed and defined so as to exclude them from immediate consideration. His strategy was simple and effective – it consisted in playing down the urgency of the Native question whilst acknowledging its importance. Union, he insisted, must come first; it was a prerequisite to a solution of the Native problem. Only a strong central Parliament, representing the collective wisdom of a great united South Africa, could produce a just and final solution of the Native problem. This became his theme song. And in presenting his point of view, he succeeded, without committing himself personally to a liberal solution, in conveying the impression that to relegate the Native problem to the future Parliament of the Union, was a wise and statesmanlike course because it would ensure a solution of which enlightened minds would approve.

Thus to Merriman, Smuts wrote as follows:

'On the question of the Native franchise my mind is full

of Cimmerian darkness and I incline very strongly to leaving the matter over for the Union Parliament . . . To us Union means more than the Native question and it will be the only means of handling the vexed question.' [11]

And to J. A. Hobson, the famous author of *Imperialism*, who was associated with a group of English M.P.s in London, and who had expressed concern about the political status of the Natives in the proposed federation or union, Smuts wrote as follows:

'My view is that the different franchise laws of the several Colonies ought to be left undisturbed and that the first Union elections ought to take place thereunder, and that the question of a uniform franchise law be gone into only after the Union has been brought about . . . you will in the Union Parliament, representing as it will all that is best in the whole of South Africa, have a far more powerful and efficient instrument for the solution of the question along broad and statesmanlike lines than you will have in the Union Convention which is going to meet next October or November. The political status of the Natives is no doubt a very important matter, but vastly more important to me is the Union of South Africa, which if not carried now will probably remain in abeyance until another deluge has swept over South Africa.' [12]

Thus Smuts's strategy was designed to ensure that the Native question, which would no doubt figure prominently in the discussions at the National Convention, would not determine the character of the Constitution. Union must come first; and however important the Native question might be, it must be treated as a separate and subordinate issue, to be finally resolved by the future parliament of the Union.

Smuts was now firmly set upon his goal of a unitary constitution. Tactically, however, he still felt the need to proceed with caution. When the more forthright Merriman submitted for his approval a draft resolution to be presented to the National Convention, asking for a legislative Union in explicit terms, Smuts sent a characteristic reply:

'I would frame the resolution so as not to arouse the fears of Natal and the Orange River Colony that unification pure and simple is intended. I would sugar the pill by referring to Provinces endowed with local self-government subject to the sovereign authority of the Union . . . I have redrafted your resolution from this point of view and think it will be more palatable to the weaker brethren.' [13]

Thus the Provincial system was conceived by Smuts, not because it had intrinsic merit, but chiefly because it would serve to propitiate Natal and the Orange River Colony. The Provincial system was a concession to federalism – but in semblance only. The Provincial Councils would be under the control of the Central Parliament; and such powers as were assigned to them could be abrogated, altered or abridged by the Central Parliament without the consent of the Provinces. The sovereignty of the Central Parliament would remain unrestricted and unimpaired.

VI

Some three months before the National Convention was due to meet, Smuts felt it was time to produce a blueprint for the proposed Union. No one else, it appeared, could or would undertake the task. Merriman was much too preoccupied with the work of the Cape Parliament, and was probably only too glad to leave the task to Smuts. Merriman, an eloquent speaker, was more at home in the debating chamber where the soaring splendour of his periods, sometimes rising to great heights, dominated the proceedings. He was content to leave the drudgery of drafting documents to others provided the work was competently done, for he had a very critical eye for slipshod work or what he called 'windy effusions'. Smuts, on the other hand, was a tireless worker; his trained, orderly and incisive mind took very readily to the work of drafting memoranda; and he no doubt knew from experience that such documents could exert a powerful influence over more indolent minds who were prone to see in a lucid, logical and well-written memorandum a fair reflection of their own thinking. He accordingly drew up a paper entitled 'Suggested Scheme for a South African Union'. He sent copies to Merriman, President Steyn (the old man was still affectionately addressed by his old title) and Sir Henry de Villiers, the Chief Justice of the Cape. In a covering letter, he told them that if the main ideas in his 'Suggested Scheme' were approved he would proceed with the drafting of a Constitution on the lines he had indicated. According to Hancock, the draft Constitution was already prepared and the 'Suggested Scheme' was in fact a summary of its main features.

Broadly speaking, they all three approved the Scheme. Each had his reservations which, however, did not affect the essential character of the political system he proposed. In essence, it was to be a unitary system, setting up a sovereign Parliament operating under a flexible Constitution.

Merriman, in his reply to Smuts, made it clear that he wanted the Cape franchise to be entrenched in the Constitution. He agreed with Smuts that each division must retain its own franchise laws; but he insisted that certain guarantees would have to be inserted in the Constitution to this effect.

President Steyn said he was largely in agreement with Smuts. On one point, however, he could not agree at all with Smuts, i.e. the point about language. He would demand equal rights to be accorded to the Dutch and English languages not only in the Courts and Parliament but also in the schools and public services.

Sir Henry de Villiers (who was destined to be the President of the National Convention) wrote, 'For the greater part it embodies my own view on the subject. I am entirely at one with you on the franchise question. This is one of the questions which will have to be relegated to the future Union Parliament . . . I am inclined to think that the British government would not object to these matters being reserved to the Parliament of United South Africa.' [14] It must be mentioned here that his advice on the subject of Union was sought and valued; it was quite in keeping with his high judicial office to give advice on the subject because the question of union was outside the realm of party politics, and he gave his advice in private so that he was not involved in public controversy.

Smuts, however, did not rely only on his draft Constitution. With characteristic foresight, he allowed himself room for manoeuvre. He prepared in addition a number of memoranda, each dealing with some specific matter, which, with intelligent anticipation, he knew would be required at various stages in the proceedings to resolve a crucial issue or elucidate a controversial point. In this he had the assistance of R. H. Brand, one of the bright young men whom Milner had recruited from Oxford and who were known, somewhat derisively, as 'Milner's Kindergarten'. And indeed Smuts made full use of the remarkable talents of Milner's young men, both in drafting constitutional ideas and propagating the cause of Union. They rendered him devoted service. Kerr edited a journal dedicated to the cause, the *State*, and Curtis made it his business to form 'Closer Union Societies', which sprang up all over the country.

As the date of the Convention approached Smuts could view the situation with satisfaction. He had laid his plans well. The stage was set for a successful Convention. He had worked out the main features of the Constitution. He had made certain through his co-operation with Merriman and President Steyn that – of the four colonies, three – namely the Transvaal, the Cape and the Orange River Colony – would on the whole favour a unitary and flexible constitution, and that together they could prevail over Natal's predilection for a federal constitution. And finally he had assembled a first-class secretariat, no less than nineteen officials, who would be at the service of the Convention, ready at all times to draft resolutions, produce memoranda, make available all required documents and render these services with faultless efficiency.

VII

The Convention duly met on 12th October.

It was fully representative of the four colonies. It was an all-White convention. The Natives of South Africa were not directly represented – their fate was to be decided for them, not by them. However, included amongst the twelve Cape delegates was W. P. Schreiner, who was an acknowledged authority on the Bantu and a staunch champion of their cause. But unfortunately Schreiner had to resign his seat to undertake the defence of Dinizulu who was standing trial for instigating the Zulu uprising of 1906. His place was taken by Colonel Stanford, a former Native Commissioner, also a champion of the Native cause, but not a federalist. Schreiner's resignation was a serious blow to the federalist cause; it meant that the Convention would include no exponent of the Cape federal point of view. It is difficult to decide how much influence he might have exerted on the other Cape delegates, but it is certain that the absence of so formidable a champion of the federal idea must have made the task of Smuts and Merriman much easier.

Sir Henry de Villiers was chosen as President of the Convention. A man of commanding presence, a jurist of great distinction and the first South African judge to serve on the Privy Council, he was held in high esteem by the British Government and was greatly respected by the delegates at the Convention. He was, moreover, no figure-head; he had a casting vote, and he could therefore play a decisive role at critical moments in the proceedings of the Convention.

In the course of his opening address Sir Henry de Villiers said:

> 'There seems to be an impression abroad that this Convention is going to lay down the lines to be followed upon such questions as to what should be the future Native policy of South Africa, but I think you will agree with me that questions of that nature can only be dealt with by us in so far as they bear upon the immediate matters submitted to our consideration.' [15]

This specific reference to the Native question, introduced in an opening address to delegates who presumably understood the purpose for which they were assembled, is highly significant. Is it not a clear indication that the Native question was uppermost in their minds – that they regarded it as the pivotal issue on which the success or failure of the Convention might turn? It seems indeed that the President's words were, in his view, necessary to put the Native question in a proper perspective; they were designed to ensure that the Native question would not dominate the proceedings, and that, in the business of constitution-making, it should be treated as a matter of subsidiary importance. The President's opening address therefore favoured the point of view of Smuts – that the merits of a unitary system as against a federal system should be debated as if the constitutional issue were unrelated to the Native question and certainly not subordinate to it.

It must be said at this stage that it is not the writer's intention to recount the history of the National Convention. He will therefore not give a blow-by-blow commentary on the debates. His purpose is to deal with the main debates, to evaluate the contributions which had a decisive or important influence on the course of these debates, and, above all, to assess the strength of the case for a unitary system as against a federal system. For an account of the proceedings the writer relies chiefly on Sir Edgar Walton's *The Inner History of the National Convention* and to a lesser extent on the *Diary* of F. S. Malan.[6]

The first debate took place on a resolution moved by Merriman, which read as follows:

A That it is desirable for the welfare and future progress of South Africa that the several British Colonies be united under one Government in a legislative union under the British Crown.

B That provision shall be made for the constitution of Provinces, with power of local legislation and administration: the present self-governing Colonies being taken as Provinces.

C That provision be made for the admission into the Union, as Provinces or Territories, of all such parts of South Africa as are not included from its establishment.

D That the Union shall be styled South Africa.

Merriman, in arguing the case against federal constitution, began with the United States, exposing what he believed to be the basic defects of the American Constitution:

'In the United States the sovereignty of the individual states was retained unimpaired . . . the people were bound to the terms of a Constitution which they were almost powerless to alter, and the principle had led to one of the greatest civil wars on record.' [16]

This broad statement, which has a semblance of plausibility, contains a contradiction. If the sovereignty of the individual states was unimpaired they could not be bound to the Federal Constitution. Their right to secede could not be questioned. In point of fact, the question of sovereignty was in dispute. There was a conflict between the Northern and Southern States on this very issue. The Northern States were influenced by Alexander Hamilton who upheld the authority of the central government. The Southern States held the Jeffersonian view that they were as free to leave the federation as they were to enter. It is, therefore, true that the immediate occasion for the quarrel which culminated in civil war was a constitutional matter, but the fundamental issue which divided the nation was the question of slavery. The issue was clearly defined by Lincoln: 'A house divided against itself cannot stand,' he declared. 'This government cannot permanently endure half slave, half free.'

Merriman then went on to discuss the Canadian Constitution:

'In Canada though the draftsmen of the Constitution had avoided some of the errors of the United States they still found that the local jealousies and differences of race and religion had prevented the achievement of a union other than imperfect. Those who had studied the Canadian Constitution and its working would agree that admirable as it was in many respects there were in it blemishes which it would be wise for South Africa to avoid. Happily for us in South Africa we had not the same obstacles to face. In religion there was no dividing line for the great bulk of the European population belonged to Protestant churches. In race the people were essentially the same and experience proved to us that the race difference was superficial and would disappear. We were therefore free from the causes which led the Canadians to secure independence to certain provinces because the Provinces differed from each other in race and religion.' [17]

Merriman was concerned exclusively with the differences between the English-speaking and the Afrikaans-speaking sections, the differences between Briton and Boer. In the light of subsequent history his prediction that these differences would disappear and the future relationship of the two groups would ensure the success of a unitary system was far too optimistic. At the time of the Convention, however, such confident predictions were understandable and could even be encouraged – were they not standing on the threshold of a new era in which the spirit of union would prevail? What is surprising is that Merriman should have ignored the differences between White and Black, differences far more pronounced than the differences between Briton and Boer.

The situation in South Africa was in fact far more complex than in Canada. In Canada the conciliation of the two White races was complicated by no Native question. Merriman had himself warned Smuts that the persistent thwarting of Native aspirations could lead to an explosive situation – he actually spoke of 'a volcano' which would 'burst forth in a destroying flood'. Merriman was then concerned with the claims of the Natives, as individuals, to the rights of citizenship. But the Natives were entitled to consideration not only as individuals; like the English-speaking and Afrikaans-speaking sections, they were entitled to consideration as ethnic groups. There were definite or clearly definable areas, occupied almost exclusively by Natives, which they could claim as their homelands; in these areas, feeling a natural urge to preserve their identity, they could legitimately aspire to self-rule. In the Transkei, the Xosas had already attained a measure of self-rule under their Bunga. A federal system would have enabled the Native ethnic groups to advance towards self-rule in their own areas and eventually receive representation in a central Parliament; it would have enabled them to determine their own future and at the same time contribute to, and participate in, the progress and prosperity of South Africa as a whole.

If the differences between the White groups made a federal constitution imperative for Canada, the wider differences between the White and Black groups made such a constitution even more imperative for South Africa. Only the fact that the National Convention was an all-White convention, confident that White ascendancy over the Native peoples could be maintained virtually for ever, can explain why, in designing a constitutional structure for the whole of South Africa, it failed to devise a constitution which would allow for the development of the Native homelands as autonomous regions within a federal framework.

Finally, Merriman felt it important to deal with the question of corruption in government.

> 'One great aim we must keep before us', continued Mr Merriman, 'was purity in our administration and the experience of the world had shown that corruption flourished more vigorously under federation than under a union government . . . if they wanted pure government they must have central control.' [18]

Purity of administration is of course immensely important. If it were true that a federal system tends to breed corruption it would be an important but not a decisive argument in favour of a unitary system. There is, however, no yardstick by which the incidence of corruption in either system can be measured and compared. In every system men must rise to positions of power, and it is power that is the corrupting factor. In a unitary system power is concentrated at the centre; and where power is the greater for being concentrated, exactions for illicit favours tend to be far more exorbitant. It is probably true to say that corruption tends to diminish in magnitude but increase in frequency as it spreads from the centre, where power is concentrated, to the periphery of the political system, where opportunities are more plentiful.

In the final analysis purity of administration depends not on the system but on the probity of the men who operate it. If all politicians were of the calibre of a Merriman the system would be above suspicion. Frequently, men, not lacking in public spirit, will try to justify their abstention from public life on the grounds that 'politics is a dirty game' or that the system breeds corruption and so forth. They cannot, however, escape responsibility for the state of affairs they condemn: for if men of integrity will not enter the political field, they leave it open to the adventurers who will not hesitate or scruple to exploit its opportunities for personal gain. Every political system must devise its own safeguards against corruption. Probably the best safeguard against corruption is a legislature, whether central or regional, which allows an opposition to operate under the rule of absolute privilege. A vigilant Opposition, itself having no favours to distribute and therefore not exposed to temptation, will be only too eager to probe and bring to the surface any evidence of nefarious practices in the governing party. And the fact that at the next election the roles may be reversed tends to have a salutary effect upon both Government and Opposition, making them both more circumspect.

Smuts then spoke, seconding Merriman's motion, and made what appears to have been the decisive speech of the debate.

'In his opening sentences', reports Sir Edgar Walton, 'General Smuts appealed to the Convention to fix their minds on great principles and not allow their work to be spoiled by too much attention to material interests or difficulties of the day . . . they were working for the future and were endeavouring to lay down a constitution which the people of South Africa would live with for many generations to come . . . In the first place they must trust the people of South Africa and they must trust each other. Distrust and suspicion would be fatal. They must also trust future South Africans, trust their wisdom, and they had no right to attempt to hamper them and bind them down by any cast-iron system or constitution which only a revolution could amend . . .' [19]

Having struck the keynote of his address, Smuts then went on to develop his argument:

'In his opinion, federation was inapplicable to South Africa.

Federation, he took it, was a treaty or pact, an agreement between independent powers. In South Africa they were not independent powers but brothers. Let them study the history of the United States of America, let them see what grave trouble had arisen purely from the nature of the constitution. Such a machinery for legislation would be unworkable in South Africa for the sovereign power was so dispersed as to be ineffective for the essential purposes of civilised government . . .

'General Smuts asked too what powers would be given to the Judiciary under federation. Are the courts to have the power to decide whether the laws passed either by the State Parliaments or by the Commonwealth Parliament are within the four corners of the constitution and if not who is to decide? Are they to leave the supreme power of government in the hands of an unrepresentative body such as a Court of Justice to over-ride an Act of Parliament? . . . A natural result of such a system was that the appointments to the Courts were political, for a political party was likely to take such precautions as were possible to insure itself and its measures against adverse judgments . . .' [20]

Smuts's main objection to a federal constitution was its rigidity which did not permit of its being amended by a simple majority. Outside of Britain, it is usual in most countries to draw a distinction between constitutional legislation and ordinary legislation. It is usual to ensure that constitutional legislation affecting the powers of the legislature and the fundamental rights and liberties of the people shall not be enacted by the ordinary procedure which requires no more than a bare majority. This distinction is based on the principle that there are matters so fundamental that it is essential in every democratic constitution to give them special protection. The legislature must not be allowed to interfere with the fundamental freedoms, such as freedom of speech and freedom of association, as easily as it interferes with the licensing laws. A Government should not be able to prolong the life of Parliament, or prevent its own dismissal, otherwise democracy would cease to exist. Ministers of State must not be placed above the law by investing them with arbitrary powers: acts of the executive power against individuals must always be subject to the scrutiny of the courts. Retrospective legislation which may condemn as criminal any act which was perfectly lawful at the time it was committed is a particularly gross violation of the rule of law. The disfranchisement of people of a particular class, colour or creed, thus excluding them from participation in government, is an outrage upon the basic concept of citizenship. All matters such as these should not be exposed to the hazards of a chance majority of the legislature. In short, a constitution which defines and places limitations on the powers of the legislature and protects the people against any invasion of their fundamental rights and liberties, should not be alterable in any respect save by a special process designed to secure general consent.

It may be argued that the Constitution of the United States, which Smuts condemned in exaggerated terms as a constitution 'which only a revolution could amend', is perhaps far too rigid, making necessary changes extremely difficult even when a convinced public opinion is in their favour. In making a new constitution, however, there is no need to follow the American precedent too closely; but the principle on which it is based should be recognised as being unassailable – no changes should be made in the constitution, the basic framework of the State, save by a process designed to secure general, as opposed to majority, consent. The constitution, which lays down a procedure for its own alteration, could adopt various devices to register general consent, e.g. a convention of the people, a special referendum, a procedure which requires a majority in excess of a bare majority in both the lower and upper houses of the central legislature, in joint or separate session, or in both the central and regional legislatures, or in a combination of these and similar devices.

Smuts was unduly perturbed about the role of the judiciary in a federal system and indeed treated it as a major objection to such a system. But obviously where a constitution defines and places limitations on the powers of the central and regional legislatures, their enactments must be subject to judicial scrutiny to ensure that they are not *ultra vires* the constitution and that the legislatures have exercised their legislative authority within their respective areas of competence. Smuts's fear was that the ruling political party would make political appointments to the courts of justice in order to protect its measures against adverse judgements. But it was surely not beyond the wit of the makers of the constitution to devise a method of appointment which would produce an independent and impartial judiciary, unaffected by political influences. One method, for example, is to make the recommendations of the Minister of Justice subject to the approval of a standing committee of judges, presided over by the Chief Justice. By some such method, immune to political interference, it should be possible to establish a judiciary above reproach in respect of merit and integrity.

Smuts then went on to urge the adoption of the British political system:

'The alternative to federation was the union as it existed in the British Islands. It was he believed the most successful system the world had ever seen and it was a model which all free people could safely copy.' [21]

The British Constitution is founded upon the unlimited sovereignty of Parliament. It draws no distinction between constitutional legislation and ordinary legislation; Parliament can change the Statutes which determine the succession to the throne in precisely the same way as it can change the licensing laws. But in lauding the British system and urging its adoption, Smuts made no mention of a highly important aspect of British constitutional practice – he said not a word about the role of convention in the working of the Parliamentary system. Convention, rooted in history or tradition, has acquired a sanctity which renders it inviolable. Convention effectively limits the sovereignty of Parliament and restricts its powers in matters of fundamental importance. Parliament as a matter of strict law can abolish the Habeas Corpus Act as easily as it can change the law relating to Summer Time; but in practice the Habeas Corpus Act enjoys the protection of a convention, rooted in tradition, which invests it with a special majesty and keeps it inviolate. It is convention that upholds the rule of law. The Civil War settled once and for all that the King is not above the law; no Parliament will therefore confer arbitrary powers upon the Sovereign or any Minister of the Crown, exempting their acts from the scrutiny of the courts, save in a national emergency and then only for the duration of the emergency. Thus, the British political system, as the result of centuries of evolution, has developed conventions which, in their practical effect, are even more efficacious than the statutory provisions which, in a rigid constitution, impose significant limits on the powers of the legislature. In a word, the British Parliamentary system is unique: it can thrive only on its own soil and in its native environment, where history has furnished it with precedents which are inviolable and tradition has established conventions which are sacrosanct.

Smuts, in urging the Convention to adopt a flexible constitution, was professing to follow the British system, but actually he went far beyond it in pursuit of flexibility. His plan, in effect, was to adopt the British Parliamentary system, to isolate it from its native environment, denude it of the conventional safeguards which limit the exercise of its legislative powers, and thus establish on South African soil a legislature whose sovereignty would be subject to no limitations whatsoever. In practice, this would mean placing an omnipotent Parliament in the hands of a ruling political party which could exercise its unfettered powers by a bare majority – an extremely hazardous experiment! It is no wonder that he appealed to the delegates to trust the people of South Africa, to trust the wisdom of the future generations. His proposal certainly called for an inordinate measure of faith and trust. If you create a political system which, with the swing of the political pendulum, will put unlimited power in the hands of your opponents, what can you rely on save faith, or perhaps the efficacy of prayer, to safeguard your position should they decide to use this power to perpetuate themselves in office and reduce all opposition, official or otherwise, to political impotence?

In constructing a political system, it is important to remember what politics is about. Politics is and has always been about power. In the beginning, men slew each other for power. At the time of the Renaissance, they used more subtle methods, such as the poisoned cup or the treacherous deed. In modern times, societies have evolved a system of rules designed to ensure that power is acquired by a more civilised process, and is exercised, not for the benefit of a privileged few, but for the common good. Smuts's exhortation, therefore, to trust the people was singularly inapt since constitutions are necessary precisely because people cannot be trusted where power is concerned. Unless it could be established that the people of South Africa differ from the rest of the human species as angels differ from men, on what conceivable grounds could one accept their trustworthiness as an adequate substitute for constitutional safeguards?

Wisdom of course is a fine attribute and doubtless the people of South Africa have their fair share of it. But unfortunately the influence of wisdom is not always manifest or decisive in the conduct of affairs. There are other human attributes – folly, self-interest, a lust for power – which are less admirable but far more prevalent than wisdom; and, unhappily, it is these less worthy attributes, these human imperfections, that are the proper concern of the constitution-maker. No constitution is deliberately designed to eliminate the operation of wisdom from the conduct of affairs – there will always be scope for its exercise. But to allow wisdom to prevail, a constitution must keep the forces inimical to wisdom firmly in check. Thus a well-designed constitution will put restraints on folly, limit the scope of self-interest and, above all, it will protect the fundamental rights and liberties of the people by imposing appropriate limitations on the exercise of power. And in a multi-racial society, a constitution based on sound principles will preclude the ruling party, representing the dominant group, from establishing a caste-dictatorship by despoiling other groups of their political rights or by denying their claim to political rights.

But such considerations, however cogent or weighty, did not trouble Smuts; he ignored them because they did not accord with his aims and ambitions – which of course is further evidence of the fact that forces other than wisdom shape the course of history. If we examine Smuts's speech in the light of subsequent history, it cannot be judged a statesmanlike performance; but addressed to a Convention consisting exclusively of White representatives its impact was overwhelming and its influence decisive. No wonder his appeal to trust the people went home! No ruling caste in history has ever recoiled from the exercise of power. It was, therefore, not difficult to persuade the Convention that in entrusting an omnipotent Parliament to a White ruling caste, they were placing it in trustworthy hands.

Merriman and Smuts, however, were not to go unchallenged. Sir Frederick Moor, the Prime Minister of Natal, put the case for federation:

'The assumption that federation was a failure was unfounded, and federation had not by any means been the failure that had been depicted. Frequent allusions had been made to the United States but he would ask them to consider the progress of that country during the past century and tell him whether the United States had not progressed enormously under federation. He did not wish to suggest to the Convention any slavish imitation of the Constitutions either of the United States or of Canada or of Australia, but he urged that they should adopt a system which would fit in with the conditions, the ideas and the genius of the South African people.' [22]

These very sensible opening remarks seemed to indicate that he sought a realistic approach to the problem of constitution-making, but, as he developed his theme, it soon became apparent that in favouring a federal system he took no account of the Native problem; so far from treating it as a matter of fundamental importance, the subject was not even mentioned. In short, Natal's preference for a federal constitution was unrelated to what Schreiner, the Cape federalist, described as 'the basic issue of Colour'.

'He agreed', Sir Frederick went on, 'that what we had in common in South Africa should be dealt with in a South African Parliament but he also contended that local Parliaments must exist for the care of local and individual interests. By all means let the rights of the local Parliaments be defined and clearly stated in the Constitution, but let there be such Parliaments and let the existing Colonies remain intact.'

Mr Morcom, who also spoke for Natal, was even more emphatic than his Prime Minister in advocating the federal system:

'Previous speakers had emphasised the differences between unification and federation. He was not prepared to enter into lengthy discussions as to the differences of meaning nor to waste time in dialectics but he would remind the delegates that they must consider the people behind them and in his opinion the people of Natal would absolutely refuse to surrender their independent powers of legislation. Natal would insist on the powers of the Central Government being clearly defined and upon wide powers being left to the local Parliaments. He spoke with a due sense of responsibility when he said Natal would insist upon this and would definitely insist upon retaining for the local Parliaments all rights and powers which were not definitely delegated to the Central Parliament and so abandoned . . . Finally Mr Morcom was strongly opposed to any measure which would tend to submerge the existing Colonies and above all there must not be even the appearance of compulsion.' [23]

Thus the case for a federal constitution was stated in very strong terms, especially by Mr Morcom. It was, however, intrinsically a weak case. It gave no clear indication as to why they wanted 'local Parliaments' and what 'local and individual interests' they wished to protect. The White settlers of Natal thought of themselves as entirely British; they were completely loyal to the Crown, deeply attached to England; and even though Natal had reached a sturdy adolescence as a self-governing colony, they wanted to maintain an umbilical relationship with the 'Mother Country'. Their spokesmen at the National Convention, however, were not worthy upholders of the British tradition of which they were so conscious. Their speeches were not on an elevated level; they derived no inspiration from the eloquence of a Burke, the compassion of a Bright, the moral fervour of a Gladstone, or the magnanimity of a Campbell-Bannerman; in their pleas there was no ringing affirmation of the values which gave worth and meaning to the British liberal tradition; there was no attempt to argue that by keeping alive this British tradition, the people of Natal would have something of value to share with others and thus make a worthwhile contribution to a wider federation. It is no wonder that their plea made no converts to the cause of federation and failed to make any impact on the National Convention.

A notable contribution to the debate was made by Mr J. W. Sauer – notable because he was the first to argue that the Native question must be treated as a factor of importance in the making of the Constitution. Sauer, one of the most stalwart of the Cape liberals, was nevertheless in favour of a unitary system and chiefly for the very reason that made Schreiner a federalist, namely an overriding concern for the rights of the Natives.

'In his opinion the differences in South Africa were mainly due to the fact that there had been different Parliaments . . . What was the paramount question in South Africa today? Would anyone deny that it was the Native question? They had a Native and Coloured population of four to one of the Whites. They had in the several Colonies different laws, regulations, rights, privileges and taxes for the Natives and the only hope of putting the Native question in South Africa on a satisfactory and permanent basis was to have one strong central Government.' [24]

Sauer wanted a unitary system because he assumed that at a later stage he, and the other Cape liberals who believed in a unitary system, would succeed in persuading the Convention to adopt their proposals for a uniform Native policy for South Africa. If he nourished such a hope he should have been quickly disillusioned by the speech of Botha which followed later:

'General Botha said he had not intervened earlier in the

debate because though he held strong views he wished to hear the discussion and consider the arguments brought forward before speaking . . . His present position was that he held himself commissioned by the Transvaal people to come to the Convention and join a Union of South Africa . . . No other form of government would in his opinion be satisfactory. The population was small and they had too few statesmen for both a Central Parliament and local Parliaments. The Transvaal would object to a number of Parliaments and what his people demanded was one flag; one people; one God . . . He did not underrate the gravity of the Native problem in South Africa but he was firmly convinced that one hope of a settlement satisfactory to both the European and the Native population was a strong central government and a uniform Native policy and Native administration throughout South Africa.' [25]

In speaking of 'one flag, one people, one God' Botha was reducing the aims of his policy of conciliation to its simplest terms. He wanted a Union, as opposed to a federation, because it would weld the Afrikaner and British elements into one harmonious nation, neither divided by conflicting loyalties nor sundered by religious differences. His conception of a united nation did not embrace the Natives and other non-Whites; when he spoke of the population of South Africa as being too small he obviously did not include them in the count. As a true descendant of the Voortrekkers he could not acknowledge that the Natives had any legitimate claim to a share in the new dispensation. Nor could Botha accept the doctrine that by enhancing the status of the Black man he would make a contribution to the progress and prosperity of the Union. The benefits of Union were for Whites only.

Both Sauer and Botha wanted a unitary system. They both wanted a uniform Native policy. They both wanted a strong central Government as the most effective method of implementing a uniform Native policy. But beyond this point came the parting of the ways. To Sauer a uniform Native policy meant that the Native's claim to political rights, fully recognised in the Cape, would receive similar recognition in the northern colonies. To Botha, a uniform Native policy meant that the northern colonies would never approve of the Cape's non-racial franchise which allowed the Natives to enjoy political rights to which, in northern eyes, they had no legitimate claim. The speeches of Sauer and Botha in this debate were a portent and a premonition of the conflict that was to develop at a later stage in the Convention.

But it should have been apparent to Sauer and the other Cape liberals even at this stage of the proceedings that there was no prospect of the Convention adopting a uniform Native policy as they understood it; and a debate on this fundamental issue would serve only to highlight the deep and irreconcilable difference of opinion between the Cape and the northern colonies. And if, to avoid a crisis, they adopted the expedient of relegating the Native question to the future Parliament of the Union, it would merely postpone or perpetuate the conflict and place the Cape non-racial franchise in jeopardy. For a sovereign Parliament (such as Sauer wanted), in which the northern colonies would have the preponderant influence, could do what the Convention was powerless to do; a sovereign Parliament could use its unfettered powers to formulate and give legislative effect to a uniform Native policy conforming to the northern tradition, which the Cape would be powerless to resist. The only safe course therefore was to refuse to accept any form of Union which did not provide an adequate safeguard for the Cape non-racial franchise – and as Schreiner insisted, the only adequate safeguard was a federal constitution.

Unfortunately, there was no one at the Convention to put the case for the federal system as Schreiner would have presented it. He might not have succeeded in influencing the final decision, but he would have added to the annals of the Convention a few honourable pages which would have given some lustre to its proceedings. For the case for federation as presented by the Natal representatives rested on nothing so fundamental as a concern for human rights. They sought merely to protect a British insularity which was more concerned with its attachment to the 'Mother Country' than its destiny in a greater South Africa. And although they argued their case in emphatic terms it all amounted to no more than a preference, and not to an uncompromising demand, for a federal system. This was proved by the fact that when the question was put and their amendment in favour of a federal constitution was defeated, they called for no division on, and therefore registered no objection to, the main resolution, now moved as a substantive motion, by Merriman and Smuts, in favour of a unitary and flexible constitution.

If Schreiner had been present he would have been resolute and uncompromising in his opposition to a unitary system. For him, fundamental human rights were the supreme consideration. A Union purchased at the expense of the rights and status of the Natives and Coloured people would have been a Union without honour. To place the Cape non-racial franchise at the mercy of a sovereign omnipotent Parliament was a betrayal of the trust which the Cape held on behalf of its non-White people. In the absence of Schreiner, the Convention was able to record a unanimous vote in favour of a unitary and flexible constitution for the Union of South Africa.

VIII

Smuts had achieved his objective. By skilful strategy he had ensured that the Native question would not influence the outcome of the debate on the form of Union; the Convention, having accepted his thesis that Union was the first priority, decided in favour of a unitary system. His triumph, however, was not yet assured. A decision on the political status of the Natives could no longer be deferred. Having decided on a unitary constitution, the Convention had now to determine the nature of the franchise provisions to be incorporated in such a constitution. This meant that the Convention would have to face the basic issue which divided the Cape from the northern colonies. Under a unitary system, how was it possible to bridge the gulf between two entirely different traditions? The Convention now entered upon the most crucial phase in its proceedings. Unless it could devise a formula to resolve the conflict of opinion which was bound to develop between the Cape and the northern colonies, the conflict, mounting to a crisis, could wreck the Convention.

Colonel Stanford began the debate by moving the following resolution:

'All subjects of His Majesty resident in South Africa shall be entitled to franchise rights irrespective of race or colour upon such qualifications as may be determined by this Convention.'

Mr Merriman thereupon moved as an amendment:

'All laws dealing with the Franchise and qualifications of electors at the date of the Union in any Colony shall remain in force until repealed or altered by the Parliament of South Africa, provided that such repeal or alteration shall be carried by a majority of not less than three-fourths of the members of both Houses sitting and voting together.'

Merriman, speaking to his amendment, 'advocated that the whole franchise question should be left as it stands, for the Union to deal with at a later date. It was useless, he said, to close one's eyes to existing facts. There were those no doubt who would be glad if they could get rid of every Black man in South Africa, but the White man found the Black man here and must take their account with him. He, Mr Merriman, was one of the Cape delegates and the Cape delegates had a special responsibility with regard to the Native and Coloured people. They were trustees for these people and had to guard the rights which had been granted to them and had not been abused. His desire was to leave the franchise as it stood in each Colony.' [26]

Merriman's amendment represented his attempt to entrench the Cape non-racial franchise in the new Constitution. Merriman's concern for the rights of the Native and Coloured people was sincere and genuine, but, unlike Schreiner, he believed that such an entrenchment written into an otherwise flexible constitution would be a sufficient safeguard for the Cape's non-racial franchise.

Colonel Stanford then spoke to his motion. His speech deserved special attention because he spoke with great authority, having been head of the Native Affairs Department in the Cape Colony for many years, and had served on the Native Affairs Commission.

'In his opinion the advance shown by the Natives during the past century had been extraordinarily encouraging. The Native had quickly grasped the advantage of civilisation and in the Transkei today the Natives had what was virtually a Native Parliament elected by themselves, consisting of Native members, raising revenue by means of taxes on Natives and carrying out much of the work of Native administration. In his opinion this progress was due to a great extent to the grant of the franchise. The Natives saw the use of the franchise and took the full benefit of it. In case of grievances they brought them before their members. The outlet for a grievance existed and it was not left to simmer in the minds of the Natives until it led to disorder and perhaps to rebellion. The experience of South Africa in this respect had been the experience of New Zealand and the experience of the United States. That experience proved there was wisdom in providing a safety-valve, in allowing a free outlet for the expression of opinion. Experience in other parts of South Africa showed that any attempt at repression was dangerous. They must realise the fact that the Natives were men and must treat them as men and slowly they would prove themselves good and worthy citizens ready and able to bear their full share of the burden of citizenship. They would take the same position and show the same progress throughout South Africa as he maintained they had done in the Cape Colony. The franchise, in his opinion, and he spoke as one who had spent his life among the Natives, was the crux of the whole Native question in South Africa and he trusted that this Convention would follow the precedent set by the United States of America and grant to Native South Africans not only freedom but citizenship.' [27]

The case for a uniform native policy throughout South Africa could not have been stated more simply and yet more effectively than in this authoritative plea of Colonel Stanford.

Sir Percy FitzPatrick, a delegate for the Transvaal, commended the principle of equal rights for all civilised men in British South Africa:

'Let them define if they could the test of civilisation and let them create a permanent tribunal which should give the necessary certificate of civilisation and he for one would support such a system.' [28]

The voice of Natal then made itself heard. Sir Frederick Moor declared that he found himself at variance with both of the two previous speakers:

'In his opinion the White and Black races in South Africa could never be amalgamated. The history of the world proved that the Black man was incapable of civilisation and the evidences were to be found throughout South Africa today. Almost every race in the world could point to its stages of civilisation but what traces of Black civilisation could South Africa produce though the Native people had been brought into contact with civilisation for ages? . . . Sir Percy FitzPatrick had spoken of a test of civilisation. What was a civilised man? Was it not a man who proved himself adaptable to a civilised community? The Natives were incapable of civilisation because they were incapable of sustained effort. He for one wanted a settlement of the question now and he felt he could speak for the Natal people. He was not prepared to leave the settlement to the Union Parliament. He would protect the native interests, he would secure them justice and freedom, but he was absolutely opposed to placing them in a position to legislate for White men.' [29]

On one point Sir Frederick agreed with Colonel Stanford and Sir Percy FitzPatrick – he wanted an immediate settlement of the question; but he wanted such a settlement to include the abolition of the Native franchise in the Cape. He should have been reminded that under a federal constitution, which he favoured, the Cape would have retained its non-racial franchise inviolate and he would have been powerless to prevent the Natives from participating in the legislative process. Equally ironical was his assertion that the Natives were incapable of civilisation because they were incapable of sustained effort, for the White settlers of Natal were notorious for their indolence – a species of languor known colloquially as 'Natal Fever' – and were completely dependent on the sustained effort of their Black workers for their comfort and prosperity. It is by such specious arguments that White supremacists seek to justify their prejudices and establish their claim to a privileged status!

Mr Abraham Fischer, speaking for the Orange River Colony,

'. . . said that the situation in South Africa in respect of this Native question seemed to him as a White man to appeal to the principle of self preservation. . . . He could ask those who knew [the Native peoples] whether they could say the Natives were fit for power? Are they fit to take part in the making of laws for South Africa? . . . A test of civilisation was spoken; what is the test of civilisation? It is not education. Not an industrial qualification. Not the improvement of property. Was it to be a liquor test? and if they granted equal rights were all prohibitions of the supply of liquor to Natives to be withdrawn? . . . Personally he would leave the question over to the Union Parliament. Only from that body could they obtain what they must have in South Africa, a uniform Native policy . . .' [30]

Mr Sauer spoke next:

'Mr Sauer declared himself in favour of equal rights and he was one of those who believed that a great principle never yet shown to have failed in the history of the world would be a safe principle in South Africa to adopt at this great moment of her life. He could not accept Sir Frederick Moor's plan because he did not believe it would lead to peace, and permanent peace could never be founded on injustice. If the delegates from the Cape advocated the Cape system it was because they spoke from experience and their experience was satisfactory . . . Granting the franchise to Natives in the Cape Colony when they had attained to a certain position and were able to pass the qualification test which their law imposed had conduced to good order in the Colony and had led the

Native people to look to Parliament for the redress of any grievance they had . . . If they were to have a contented country the interests of all must be represented in the Parliament of the country and there must be political equality. Men talked of social equality. That was beside the question, it was not a matter that Parliament could decide for the people nor was there social equality among Whites in any civilised country. That was one of the things people settled for themselves . . . He had heard something of a civilisation test . . . By all means let them fix a standard, a qualification for the franchise but when they had fixed it let them bar none who can pass it . . . Justice could not be tampered with with impunity and justice to the Natives would secure the position of the White man in South Africa for all time . . . We could not govern the Natives fairly and justly unless they were represented by their own elected representatives . . . Had they considered too the danger of living among a numerically stronger class of people to whom they denied the rights and privileges of citizenship? Where was the people in the history of the world who had not sunk to the level of those they held in subjection? . . . In the Cape the Natives and Coloured people were more content than in any other portion of the British Empire. The Cape had proved the success of its principles and had the right to ask for the adoption of its policy by South Africa.' [31]

At this stage of the debate, the lines of battle having been clearly drawn, Smuts no doubt felt that this was the strategic moment for his intervention. 'He at once declared that much as he sympathised with Mr Sauer's argument he feared that the enunciation of high principles would not lead them to the solution of the practical problem which they had to face.'

Smuts, it will be recalled, in the debate on the form of the constitution, had begun his speech by exhorting the delegates 'to fix their minds on high principles': he now felt that 'high principles' were an encumbrance when dealing with a matter of such fundamental importance as the Native question. They must abjure high principles; they must be pragmatic; they must concern themselves with what is politically feasible. That was now the key-note of his address to the Convention.

'It was true', Smuts said, 'that in the Cape they had experimented with the principles of giving the franchise to Natives on the same conditions as to White men. Even in the Cape he believed opinions differed as to the effects of that experiment and it would be agreed that their experience in South Africa was limited. They could not hope, sitting there for a few weeks or months as the case might be, to evolve a satisfactory solution of all the problems of South Africa and he thought that this was one of the problems they should leave for future solution. The Convention he feared would not be able to solve the two problems of Union and the Native question. There were four solutions open to them:

i. To adopt the Cape Franchise for the whole of South Africa.
ii. To fix a civilisation test for all Natives and persons of colour.
iii. To draw a hard and fast colour line throughout the Union.
iv. To leave the position in the Cape as it now stands and allow the Union Parliament to settle the question at some future date.

With regard to the first proposal, namely to adopt the Cape franchise for the Union, it was impossible for the people would not accept it and the Constitution would be rejected. With regard to the second the Cape would have great trouble with its Coloured voters and its adoption might lead to the rejection of the Constitution by the Cape, while its fate would certainly be jeopardised in the Transvaal and Orange River Colony; the third he was not in favour of but he would recommend the fourth to their consideration.' [32]

To sum up, Smuts wanted the franchise to be left as it stood in the Cape, but that it be left to the Union Parliament to amend it by a simple majority. He was not even in favour of Mr Merriman's amendment which aimed at the entrenchment of the Cape franchise. Smuts must have known that to leave the question to be decided by a simple majority in the future Union Parliament would be to doom the Cape Native franchise to an early extinction.

At this stage, the President, Sir Henry de Villiers, deemed it important to intervene and made a significant statement:

'He said there were certain aspects of the case which it would be well for them to have before them while coming to a decision. He was recently in England and had the opportunity of discussing the objects of the Convention with leading men there. He found them all willing to give a free hand to South Africans to arrange matters in their own way, but they excepted two questions, that of the Native franchise and the control of the Protectorates.[7] To both these points the greatest importance was attached and the Imperial Government regarded itself in a special sense as guardian and trustee for the Natives in South Africa . . . If the settlement of the franchise question was regarded as unsatisfactory by the Imperial Government then the Protectorates would not be handed over. It was desired also to fix such a standard of qualification for the franchise as would leave the door open for the Natives to qualify for full rights of citizenship . . . His own opinion was that it would be wise to consult the Imperial Government before taking decisive action. And he would remind them that their Constitution when passed and approved by South Africa must be passed and approved by the British Government and British Parliament which must pass an Imperial Act. The South African Colonies had no power to do that. Lord Selborne's suggestion was for the creation of an impartial board which should apply a test of civilisation to Coloured applicants for the franchise . . . If however the majority of the delegates were of opinion that such a suggestion would jeopardise the Constitution then the Imperial Government would agree to leave the Cape franchise as it was provided it could not be altered detrimentally to the Coloured voters by a majority of less than three-fourths of the two Houses of Parliament sitting together while for an extension of the franchise to other parts of the Union only a bare majority should be sufficient.' [33]

Whether the President's introduction had any decisive influence on the delegates it would be hard to say, but his reminder that the Imperial Government was concerned about the fate of the Natives and that its attitude could not be ignored was no doubt designed to ensure that a spirit of compromise would prevail; and he even indicated the lines on which he felt a compromise solution might be sought.

General Hertzog, however, was not prepared to compromise:

> 'General Hertzog could not shake himself free of the anxiety he felt in regard to this question and he saw great danger ahead if once the principle were adopted of giving votes to the Natives. There would be constant pressure to lower the qualification standard and in the near future the Native voter would swamp the European. He could not see his way to agree to any of the suggestions in that direction . . .' [34]

Mr F. S. Malan then spoke:

> 'It was of great importance, he said, to try and find a general solution for this difficult problem; and only if it should prove impossible to find such a solution, acceptable to the people and also not endangering the Union, could one think of a temporary solution such as advocated by Mr Merriman . . . The danger of putting off the finding of a uniform system was:
>
> (*i*) that the Europeans would remain divided on this point and that this division would be transferred to the Union.
>
> (*ii*) that in addition it would make a poor impression on the Natives, as it would cause a feeling that they had been unjustly treated and a feeling of dissatisfaction in the Provinces where they – the Natives – were disfranchised . . .
>
> He suggested that the Native should obtain a certificate showing that he was competent to be regarded as a citizen before he could become a voter. Just as a foreigner had to obtain a naturalisation certificate so the Native should first obtain a certificate of citizenship. As regards the qualifications for European and Native citizens no difference should be made. Along these lines the colour bar would be avoided and at the same time the abuses would be prevented.' [35]

General Botha entered the debate to define the attitude of his Government:

'General Botha feared that there was no hope of a final solution of this thorny question being reached by the Convention now. Their first duty as a Convention was to draw up a Constitution for a united South Africa and Colonel Stanford's resolution if passed would, he feared, ruin the object which the Convention had in view. Their first duty was to bring about the union of the White races in South Africa and after that it would be possible to deal with the Native population . . . In his opinion if vested interests were safeguarded that was as far as they could go but on one point there must be no manner of doubt – they could only have Europeans in Parliament . . . He could only repeat that in his opinion an attempt at a final solution now could only have the effect of wrecking the object which the union had in view . . . At the same time he would leave the Cape as it stood and not interfere with the franchise now enjoyed by the Coloured people there. They had great difficulties to face in the Transvaal already before Union was accepted by the people and he could assure the delegates that if he had to tell the electors that they must accept the principle of the Native franchise his position would become impossible.' [36]

General de Wet then rose to state that he was in thorough agreement with General Botha. General de Wet spoke with the authentic voice of the Voortrekker:

'Providence had drawn the line between Black and White and we must make that clear to the Natives and not instil into their minds false ideas of equality. In his opinion that was the greatest kindness and the greatest justice we could do them. In the Cape Colony they had followed a different principle and he considered that the Native of the Cape Colony had been made unhappy by the attempt to put him on a platform to which he did not belong. He warned them to deal cautiously with this question for if he knew the feeling of the country they might wreck the whole Convention through it.' [37]

The cleavage between the Cape and the northern colonies now stood clearly revealed. It was deep and unbridgeable. Some delegates felt that the Convention had reached an impasse – was there any point in continuing? In the tense atmosphere, Mr Malan rose for the second time to make an impassioned plea:

'. . . he regarded it as his duty to make a last earnest appeal to the Convention to try and arrive at a uniform system. This was a crisis in the history of the people of South Africa. It had taken a hundred years of strife and wars to bring the Europeans to unification. By not facing squarely the disagreement over the Natives they were once again heading for a struggle and tears and suffering. People spoke about the necessity to unite the White races first and then to tackle the Native franchise question, but a union of this kind would not be a genuine union. The germs of discord would continue to exist. It had been suggested that only the descendants of Europeans should be allowed as members of the Union Parliament. This was a curtailment of the rights which had already been enjoyed by the Native voters in the Cape Colony . . . How could he vote for it without giving these same voters something in exchange. What would be the first question that would be put to the leaders of the Cape Colony; this, whether they were in favour of the extension of the franchise in the other parts of the Union. It was in the interests of the Europeans of South Africa that an attempt should be made not only to obtain a uniform system for the whole of South Africa, but also to put the system of the Cape Colony on a sound basis. The present was the best possible time.' [38]

Botha rose immediately to reply to Malan. His speech was terse and uncompromising. It heightened the tension:

'General Botha said that Malan's speech had made him fear for Union because he saw in it a desire to force the rest of South Africa to accept the principle of the Native franchise of the Cape Colony. If this were done he might just as well go home. He would not go further than the recognition of the rights of the Natives in the Cape Colony.' [39]

In this atmosphere of crisis Mr Sauer moved the adjournment of the debate, presumably to allow for a cooling-off period or perhaps to indicate that a deadlock had been reached and that it was useless to continue a fruitless discussion. The Convention, however, was determined to bring the issue to a vote and the motion was negatived. Botha, however, saved the situation by moving that a Committee be appointed to deal with the whole question of the franchise.

For ten days the Committee was immersed in the problem of the Native franchise, debating every aspect of the momentous issue. The Cape delegates exerted themselves to obtain the vote for all Natives, throughout the Union, on the basis of a civilisation test. They fought in vain; in the end they had to concentrate their efforts on retaining the vote for the Native and Coloured men of the Cape. Eventually, however, on the basis of the Committee's recommendations, the Convention adopted the following compromise:

1. Voting rights as they existed in each Colony to remain in force.
2. Entrenchment of the Cape non-racial franchise which could be altered only by a two-thirds majority of both Houses of Parliament in joint session.
3. Only persons of European descent could be eligible for membership of either of the Houses of Parliament.

Thus the Native voters and the Coloured voters of the Cape remained on the Common roll. But they retained only the right to vote. They were no longer eligible for election to Parliament. By making this surrender of principle the Cape drove a deep fissure into its basic structure of equality.

The Cape delegates to the Convention, however, refused to see it as a betrayal of trust. They had agreed to this surrender of principle reluctantly and from the best of motives; they had to agree to it as a necessary part of the compromise without which Union could not have been achieved. At least, they had succeeded in entrenching the Cape non-racial franchise, thus safeguarding it for all time – so they believed.

Having accepted the compromise – known as the 'Grand Compromise' because it enabled Union to come into being – the Cape sought consolation in the belief that the march of progress would ensure the ultimate triumph of the Cape liberal tradition. Sauer said at the time, 'I hope that when we get Union we shall approach nearer eventually to the aim of equality. I believe . . . you will be able to introduce your policy into the other parts of South Africa.' It was true they had surrendered a basic principle in order to achieve the all-important goal of Union. It was therefore not so much a surrender as a strategic retreat. From the secure base of its entrenched position in the Cape, liberalism could now survey a far wider area open to its advance. The spirit of the times encouraged this belief. The nineteenth century had been the epoch of liberal triumph; no other doctrine spoke with the same authority or exercised such a wide-spread influence. Its force was not spent; there was no reason why it should not advance to even greater triumphs in the new century. Under the British Crown – which owed its lustre to the fact that it was the symbol of the British liberal tradition – liberalism had taken deep root in the Cape. In a united South Africa under the British Crown liberal institutions would prosper as they had prospered in the Cape. Above all, the values which gave worth and meaning to their liberal philosophy were imperishable and as long as they remained faithful to these values the ultimate triumph of their cause was assured. This was the theme of much inspired rhetoric in the Cape.

Only one man refused to be beguiled. Schreiner refused to accept the compromise. He had no faith in the power of liberalism to convert its opponents in the future when it had failed so conspicuously to influence them in the past. The Constitution – the South Africa Act – he described not as an Act of Union but rather as an Act of Separation between the minority and the majority of the people of South Africa. He denounced the exclusion of non-White members from the Union Parliament. As for the entrenchment of Cape franchise, he attached no value to it. Indeed he condemned the entrenchment as a trap. He warned those who had faith in its efficacy as a safeguard that northern opinion would remain forever intransigent and hostile to the Native franchise – it followed therefore that if only a small number of Cape representatives in the Union Parliament betrayed their trust,

'Native and Coloured Parliamentary rights would vanish into thin air under Parliamentary sanction.' [40] Subsequent history shows how right Schreiner was.

IX

At the end of the Convention there was a moment of soul-searching. F. S. Malan moved that the following words be inserted in the preamble of the Constitution: 'trusting in the guidance and blessing of God Almighty'. There were objections. Mr Fischer 'did not want such holy words to appear in an Act'. General Hertzog 'did not want to be accused of hypocrisy through the insertion of these words'. Mr Merriman 'felt that he could not insert these words as a colour bar had been drawn in the Constitution'. On a division the motion was defeated by sixteen votes to thirteen. The blessing of God Almighty could not be invoked. [41]

But General Smuts had no problem of conscience. As far as he was concerned the Constitution had been handed down from Sinai. 'The Constitution', he said, 'is not a man's work. It bears the impress of a Higher Hand.' [42]

Mrs Millin, who records these words, cannot avoid the conclusion that Smuts was the instrument of the Higher Hand. In the making of the Constitution, Smuts's role was similar to the role played by James Madison, known as 'the Father of the American Constitution', at the Philadelphia Convention. He had, as his biographer Hancock says, 'planned from start to finish the strategy and tactics that dominated the campaign for Union'. At the Convention itself he had not only influenced the course of the debates, intervening effectively at crucial moments, finding ingenious compromises to end a deadlock, producing memoranda and drafting appropriate resolutions; he had, in a word, masterminded the whole proceedings of the Convention, always on the alert, always ready with fertile expedients. But as the instrument of the Higher Hand he occasionally displayed an excess of zeal. Sir Percy FitzPatrick says in a private letter:

'Smuts has been twice caught and exposed in deliberate

trickery, phrasing his resolutions with amazing cleverness so that they can mean the very opposite of what he appears to concede. But he has no feeling of shame or resentment and resumes at once his too perfect air of camaraderie and overdone boyish frankness. By two wanton and short-sighted acts of duplicity he has managed to give every man in the Convention the same feeling of profound mistrust that dogs him in all he does. It is wonderful that so clever a man should not be clever enough to be reasonably straight.' [43]

Professor Thompson believes that FitzPatrick's letter referred to two episodes: (1) Smuts's conduct when the first report on the franchise was before the Convention; (2) Smuts's amendment for the readjustment of Provincial representation in the House of Assembly. Hancock, however, suggests that FitzPatrick greatly exaggerated what actually happened. 'FitzPatrick', he says, 'was a pugnacious, romantic, lovable Irishman who always saw everything in black and white and had a great gift for fluent and vivid prose portraiture, or caricature.' He maintained that Smuts was 'slim' in the good but not in the bad sense of the word. 'Nobody, surely,' says Hancock, 'wants stupid soldiers and naive politicians: one wants them to be single- but not simple-minded: one wants them to be men of honour but also men of resourcefulness, ingenuity, technical dexterity.' [44] What Hancock appears to be saying is that the politician, like the practitioner of sleight-of-hand, is entitled, by right of his profession, to practise deception without loss of honour. It is, however, the essence of the illusionist trick that it should escape detection – and in this respect it appears that Smuts was not always successful.

Smuts's 'slimness' however manifested itself in even more important matters than in the drafting of ambiguous and deceptive resolutions. He was not averse to speaking with two voices. Thus when he sought to influence Hobson and his group of English M.P.s, he wrote as follows:

'When Union has been brought about, and supposing it assumes the form of unification . . . a general franchise law for South Africa will become necessary. And it seems to me that the great probability is in favour of a simple manhood suffrage for all Whites such as we have now in the Transvaal and Orange River Colony. Now evidently the franchise could be conferred on the Native population also. Manhood suffrage for the Whites would inevitably mean a different franchise for Natives. And I think such a differential franchise could be justified on the strongest grounds. In other words any Native franchise will have to contain certain tests of education and civilised life which could not be applied to the Whites. What these tests are to be I do not consider it above the wit of man to determine . . .' [45]

In commending the draft Constitution to the Transvaal Legislature for its approval, Smuts spoke as follows:

'Every attempt was made in the Convention in order to have a uniform system of franchise in South Africa, but it was found to be impossible. It was only after much discussion and probing into this most difficult problem that it was found impossible to abolish the Native franchise in the Cape. Nor could we find an alternative solution . . . All we could do was to admit our inability to remove it. We have to admit that and that it is for the future South Africa to remove it.' [46]

Which of these two utterances, completely contradictory, represented the true Smuts? Which was the mask and which was the face? We shall never know. We shall never 'pluck the heart of his mystery'. We shall certainly not arrive at the truth by weighing one statement against another, balancing one declaration against its opposite. Smuts was a complex personality; his inner motives, the concealed springs of action, are not really the concern of the historian. It is the business of his biographer to unravel the enigma – if he can. As Hancock rightly points out, a politician must be effective; and although his motives and methods will undoubtedly influence his conduct of affairs, either enhancing or inhibiting his effectiveness, it is by his actual achievements that a politician must be judged. No politician could be more 'slim' than Talleyrand, yet he served his country through many vicissitudes and served it well – perhaps because of his 'slimness'. The historian, as distinct from the biographer, will attempt the less baffling and more rewarding task of making an assessment, in terms of success or failure, of the role history will assign to Smuts.

X

In addressing the Transvaal Legislature, Smuts's speech, indicating that the abolition of the Cape Native franchise was a task for the future, was of course well attuned to the feelings of its members, whose approval he sought for the draft Constitution. Other politicians repeated his views in even more intransigent terms. It was regrettable that the Cape was allowed to retain the Native franchise, even more regrettable that the Convention had to agree to its entrenchment. However, the Cape Native franchise, despite its entrenchment, was only a temporary blot on the Constitution; it would be expunged as soon as the north could make its more robust standpoint prevail over the misguided liberalism of the Cape. In short, the northern politicians were making statements in direct conflict with those which Merriman and his colleagues were making in the Cape. Merriman was compelled to write to Smuts, imploring him not to use arguments in the Transvaal which would damage his own arguments in the Cape. 'All our speeches are boomerangs – what is received with applause in Cape Town is anathema in Pretoria and vice versa.' [47] Merriman no doubt feared that their speeches would have a reciprocal effect in damaging each other's attempt to secure approval for the draft Constitution in their respective legislatures.

It was clear that the National Convention had produced a compromise which could do no more than render the Constitution immediately acceptable, and thus enable Union to come into being. The Convention could not resolve the basic issue which divided the Cape from the northern colonies. In the ensuing clash of ideologies, the northern politicians were destined to prove themselves more resolute and dynamic in the pursuit of their aim, as Schreiner had foreseen. There was hardly a period of truce. The Union was scarcely established – the honeymoon period was not yet over – when the north began to drive for a uniform Native policy. Such a uniform Native policy, conforming of course to the northern outlook, would have to be based on the principle of segregation. The Natives Land Act of 1913 represented the first stage in the implementation of such a policy. The Act made it illegal for Natives to purchase land outside the existing reserves and such additional areas as the Government would demarcate for Native occupation.

The movement for a uniform Native policy received a fresh impetus when a decision of the Supreme Court laid down that the Natives of the Cape Province were exempted from the Act and retained complete freedom to buy land anywhere in the Cape because the purchase of land was one of the methods by which the Natives could qualify as voters in the Cape. This decision created an intolerable situation. If the Natives in the Cape could qualify for the common roll, they could never be relegated to separate areas; territorial segregation would be impossible. Moreover, the day would surely come when the Black voters on the common roll would outnumber the White voters, and that of course would mean the end of White supremacy, and the doom of White civilisation in South Africa. The only solution was to abolish the Cape Native franchise. To maintain White supremacy, political power must remain in White hands and must be used to enforce a policy of segregation. Thus a uniform Native policy, of which White supremacy was the governing principle, could obviously not tolerate the Cape Native franchise. Unfortunately it had been entrenched in the Constitution, but as soon as the requisite two-thirds majority could be achieved the Cape Native franchise would have to go.

XI

'Trust the people of South Africa,' said General Smuts, when he urged the National Convention to adopt a unitary and flexible constitution. 'We must trust future South Africans, trust their wisdom.'

Let us now see, in the light of subsequent history, whether his faith in the trustworthiness of the people into whose hands the Constitution was delivered, was justified. Let us see whether his faith in the wisdom of future generations was vindicated.

A brief summary of events, some of which will be dealt with in detail in subsequent sections, will at this stage serve to instruct the reader.

In 1933 General Hertzog and General Smuts joined forces to form a coalition Government and subsequently fused their respective parties to form the United Party. General Hertzog made it a condition of fusion that his Native Bills, which according to him constituted a final settlement of the Native problem, should receive prior treatment. One of these measures, the Natives Representation Bill, was designed to remove the Cape Natives from the common roll. As a result of fusion, Hertzog now had an opportunity of obtaining the two-thirds majority in a Joint Sitting of both Houses required by the Constitution to secure the enactment of the Bill. Hertzog had intended originally to abolish the Cape Native franchise, but in order to reduce resistance to his measure he decided, as a compromise, to place the Cape Native voters on a separate roll and to give them the right to elect three White representatives to Parliament. The compromise was of no great value to the Cape Natives, for the purpose of a separate roll was to segregate them from the main body of voters, turn them into a permanent political minority and reduce them to political impotence. Hertzog presented the Natives Representation Bill to Parliament in 1936. Although it was agreed that those M.P.s and Senators who had scruples of conscience about the measure were free to speak and vote against it, the Bill was passed by an overwhelming majority – 169 voted for the Bill and only 11 voted against it. Schreiner's prophecy was fulfilled. Only 4 Cape M.P.s and 1 Cape Senator refused to betray their trust; all the rest voted with the great majority. Thus in the year 1936 the 'Grand Compromise' which had made Union possible was destroyed.

Next came the turn of the Coloured people. In 1948 the Nationalist Party under Dr D. F. Malan came to power with a very narrow majority – a majority of five over all the opposition parties. The immediate concern of the Nationalist

Government was to strengthen its position and entrench itself in office. Dr Malan suddenly discovered that the growth of the Coloured population constituted a grave danger to White civilisation. He pointed out that in the Cape there were already more Coloured children in the schools than White children. It was therefore imperative to sunder the Coloured voters from the main body of voters and give them a limited number of representatives – White representatives of course – in both the Senate and Lower House.

It was no use reminding Dr Malan that General Hertzog and other leaders of the Nationalist Party had given a solemn pledge to the Coloured people that their political rights would always be respected. Dr Malan said that in view of the grave danger to White civilisation they could not allow themselves to be 'ruled by the dead hand of the past'. The fact that the Coloured vote could decide the fate of a number of Cape constituencies and that the elimination of the Coloured voters from the common roll would enable the Nationalists to win or retain a number of seats was, of course, purely coincidental. To remove the Coloured voters from the common roll, he was prepared to plunge the country into a constitutional crisis. The Nationalists could not command the two-thirds majority in a Joint Sitting required in terms of the entrenched clauses of the Constitution. They argued that it was not necessary; the Statute of Westminster and the Status of the Union Act of 1934 had conferred full sovereign independence on South Africa, and its Parliament could now determine its own procedure and pass by a simple majority any law, whether or not it offended against the entrenched clauses.[8]

The Opposition, however, insisted upon the moral aspect of the Constitutional issue: irrespective of the legal aspect, there were three powerful reasons why the entrenched clauses should be treated as sacrosanct. Firstly, without the entrenched clauses Union could never have taken place; they therefore had the force and validity of a solemn compact, as binding as a Treaty obligation. Secondly, after the Statute of Westminster, in 1931, the validity of the entrenched clauses was reaffirmed by a special resolution of both Houses, and it was solemnly declared to be a matter of honour to keep them inviolate. Thirdly, the requirements of the entrenched clauses were scrupulously respected in the passing of the Native Legislation of 1936, a procedure which established a Parliamentary precedent. Thus obligation, honour and precedent combined to make the entrenched clauses absolutely inviolable. Despite all this, the Government went ahead with its measure, the Coloured Voters Bill,[9] which was passed in both Houses by a simple majority. The United Party Opposition immediately challenged the validity of the measure in the Courts; and the highest legal authority in the land, the Appeal Court, ruled that the Coloured Voters Act was unconstitutional and therefore invalid. The decision of the Appeal Court forced the Government to accept the legal validity of the entrenched clauses; but nothing can absolve it from an act of perfidy which made it necessary to invoke the Courts.

The Government, however, would not accept defeat. Dr Malan introduced a Bill to establish a 'High Court of Parliament' – making Parliament itself a court, higher than the Appeal Court, which would give the final decision on all constitutional matters. The Bill was duly passed. The 'High Court of Parliament' assembled. The Opposition parties would, of course, have no part in it and absented themselves. And the High Court of Parliament in solemn session duly validated the Coloured Voters Bill. What Dr Malan did, in effect, was to clothe the Nationalist Party caucus in the trappings of a judiciary, parade it as a High Court of Parliament, and make it deliver a pre-determined judgment on its own previous efforts at law-breaking! What is there to say of a Government which could stoop to such a transparent imposture? Dr Malan has probably earned a unique place for himself in history. Caligula made his horse a consul, the Emperor Heliogabalus made his ballet-mistress commander of the Praetorian Guard, and a King Henry of France is reputed to have made his barber High Chancellor of the Realm; but these potentates never attempted anything so wholesale and spectacular as the elevation of a motley throng of party hacks to the position of judges at the summit of an otherwise impeccable judicial system. It should be noted, however, that with the exception of the horse, all these high dignitaries had one thing in common – they had a blind and unquestioning obedience to the dictates of their masters as their sole qualification for exalted office.

The validity of the High Court of Parliament was duly challenged. The Appeal Court pronounced it invalid. Its finding, in effect, was that the High Court of Parliament was a nullity constituting itself an entity.

The attempted rape of the Constitution failed. The Appeal Court had rendered the entrenched clauses inviolate. But the ingenuity of the Government was by no means exhausted. It passed a Bill, by a simple majority, to enlarge the Senate, adding a sufficient number of Senators to give it the necessary two-thirds majority in the Joint Sitting. This time the Appeal Court ruled that the measure was valid. The packed Senate duly gave the Government the necessary two-thirds majority – the Coloured voters were removed from the common roll.

Thus a measure, passed by a simple majority, enabled the Government to fabricate an artificial two-thirds majority and achieve its purpose. The fact that the Constitution could not forbid such a stratagem exposed the utter absurdity of writing an entrenchment into an otherwise flexible constitution – an absurdity on a par with an attempt to safeguard one's home by bolting the front door and leaving the windows wide open! A rigid constitution – a constitution in which every clause is entrenched – would have provided no loophole through which the provisions safeguarding the political rights of the Coloured people could have been circumvented.

The rest of the story is quickly told. The Nationalist Government, now fully in command of the requisite two-thirds majority, could proceed with the completion of its programme. In 1956 a Bill was passed in a Joint Sitting to repeal the entrenchment of the Native Representation. In 1959 a Bill abolished all Native Representation in Parliament. And finally the Coloured Representation was abolished, for no more valid reason – not disclosed of course – than that the newly formed Progressive Party would probably win the four Coloured seats. Thus the Government reached the inevitable conclusion – completely logical in terms of its political philosophy – that the most effective way to eliminate an opposition was to use the exorbitant powers placed in its hands by a Sovereign Parliament to disfranchise those who were not prepared to accept its policies. Would the process end with the exclusion of the non-White opposition groups?

XII

The Hertzog legislation of 1936 was epoch-making. It accomplished far more than the removal of the Native voters from the common roll. It initiated a process which not only deprived the Natives and Coloured people of their political rights, but produced a change in the character of Parliament itself. For once it was finally established that distinctions of race or colour were legitimate grounds for the denial of political rights, Parliament faced a situation which offered a serious challenge to its continued existence as a representative institution. The 1936 legislation was enacted at a time when Parliament, if it was to continue as a representative institution, should have been ready to adapt itself to a changing social structure. Rapid industrial development, gathering momentum, was drawing the Natives into the urban areas, and establishing them as a permanent part of the industrial labour force. This process represented a potential challenge to White supremacy for sooner or later a great Black proletariat, conscious of its vital importance to the economy, would demand its rightful place in the system of Parliamentary representation. Clearly, if Parliament continued to deny the great bulk of the population any share in political power when they were ripe for emancipation, it would cease to be a representative institution and would become in fact the stronghold of a White oligarchy.

Under Nationalist rule, Parliament has undergone a significant change in this direction. Parliament has in fact become the close preserve of a White ruling caste whose chief preoccupation is the making of laws designed to maintain White supremacy. As the stronghold of an exclusive oligarchy it must inevitably provoke the hostility of the non-White masses who are debarred from its privileges. To safeguard their monopoly of political power the White ruling caste have adopted to an increasing extent an authoritarian technique. They continue, of course, to use the established procedures of Parliament to give legal force to their decisions; but, in essence, Parliament has ceased to be a representative institution resting upon the consent of the governed – it has become the law-making instrument of a ruling caste and its legislation tends to become more and more coercive in character.

It is significant that the Nationalist Government no longer keeps up even the pretence of consulting the Natives in the making of laws which vitally affect them. One of the first acts of the Government was to abolish the Native Representative Council, set up under the 1936 legislation as an advisory body to be consulted on all measures affecting Native interests. As it could no longer serve a useful purpose as a consultative body, its abolition, from the point of view of the Government, was a logical and necessary step. The policy of apartheid provides no basis for consultation. It would be a futile procedure to seek the co-operation of the Natives in the making of laws which are designed to maintain White domination and to enforce, in every possible sphere, a master–servant relationship between White and Black. Apartheid laws must be imposed from above, without consultation and certainly without the consent of the governed. To set up machinery of consultation would merely impede the operation of Parliament as the coercive law-making instrument of the ruling caste.

The Nationalist Government, however, can afford to preserve Parliament as a democratic facade for its authoritarianism; having a docile and submissive majority at its command and being subject to no constitutional restraints, the Government still finds it convenient to make use of Parliament in order to give legislative force to its decrees, and the debates enable it to explain and publicise its measures.

In 1948, immediately after the Nationalist Party's accession to power, the Labour Party moved a resolution asking the Government 'to give an undertaking that it will in no way infringe such democratic rights and freedoms as are at present enjoyed by the people of South Africa'. Dr Malan, the Prime Minister, replied to the debate. He strongly resented the suggestion that his Government was not entirely democratic. He behaved as Caesar would have behaved if someone had ventured to suggest that his wife was not entirely above suspicion. But despite this show of indignation, he gave the undertaking. He affirmed his fidelity to what he called the 'Western conception of democracy' and went on to define it in some detail:

'We also stand for the Western conception of democracy . . . The Western conception is that in the first instance we must bear in mind the rights and freedom of the individual. The individual has human rights and nothing should be allowed to infringe upon his human rights . . . The individual has the right to live; he has the right of physical movement, of action. He has the right of freedom of thought; he has the right of exercising a free conscience; he has the right to freedom of religion; he has the right to express himself and his opinions. He can do so in public life where he takes part in the politics of his country. He can do so through the press; he can do so by taking part in the political struggle. He can call into being political parties and in that way join issue in public life with others whose views differ from his.' [48]

This was Dr Malan's assurance. The rights and freedoms which he set forth in this solemn affirmation are the very essence of the democratic system and could not be defined in more precise terms. According to Western conceptions of Government, these rights and freedoms are inalienable; they constitute as firm a basis for the democratic way of life as the solid ground beneath one's feet.

But all the fundamental rights and freedoms which Dr Malan affirmed so solemnly have consistently been violated by the Nationalist Government of which he was Prime Minister. The individual, about whom he was so concerned, no longer enjoys these freedoms as a matter of right but only on sufferance. He enjoys them at the whim of a Government which has gathered the most despotic and far-reaching powers into its hands. The Suppression of Communism Act – the first and still the most notorious of its reactionary measures – places the Government above the law. This Act is ostensibly aimed at 'Communists' but its definition of Communism is so wide and the powers it confers on the Government so arbitrary, that it can be used against anyone who opposes Government policy. Under this Act, the Government, by executive action alone, can eliminate an opponent from the political field and liquidate the political party to which he belongs. It can strip him of his civic rights, remove him from public office, deprive him of his livelihood, and banish him from his home. It can place him under house arrest and restrict his movements. It can suppress any newspaper of which it disapproves, and it can ban any publication it dislikes. And by virtue of the retrospective provisions of the Act, it can take this drastic action against a person whose conduct before the Act came into force was perfectly lawful and whose behaviour ever since has been impeccable.

There are no safeguards against the abuse of these arbitrary powers; there is no right of appeal to the Courts. These exorbitant powers were conferred on the Government by a ruling party which tends to equate itself with the state as a whole, and tends, therefore, to regard any opposition, especially to apartheid, as a form of treason.

But the most ferocious of the Government's Draconian measures is the Terrorism Act. In terms of this Act the police can at any time arrest anyone without stating reasons and can suspend Habeas Corpus for 180 days. Unlimited authority is conferred on the arresting official, and detainees are held in solitary confinement, without visitors or reading or writing material, in a state of almost continual deprivation. On the termination of the 180 days he can be arrested for successive periods of 180 days if the police deem fit. Mr Vorster, the Prime Minister who was responsible for this measure, declared that he had the power to detain a person for as long as he liked this side of eternity. Perhaps he deserves to be commended for his moderation in refraining from extending his authority into the next world.

Thus Parliament, operating under a flexible constitution, has invested the executive with powers which place it above the law. Rule by executive decree has superseded the rule of law. And the White electorate have been conditioned to accept every piece of authoritarian legislation, however drastic and despotic, because it is in essence an apartheid measure – it is designed to safeguard White supremacy and to keep the Black man in his place. The electorate are prepared to acquiesce in such legislation even if it restricts the rights and liberties of the White man as well. To submit to authoritarian rule may be irksome but it is the price the White man is prepared to pay for the maintenance of his privileged status.

XIII

In the light of subsequent history, it is no exaggeration to say that the National Convention made a disastrous choice when it decided in favour of a unitary and flexible constitution. If Schreiner's plea for a federal system had prevailed, the whole course of history would have been altered. The Cape – the largest and, in terms of civilised values, the most mature of the four Provinces – would have preserved its non-racial franchise. It would not have been rendered powerless to resist the reactionary tide which, sweeping down from the north, has extinguished every trace of the liberal tradition it brought into the Union.

History has vindicated Schreiner's standpoint, but what is its verdict on Smuts? It may be argued that Smuts was no reactionary, that basically he respected the democratic process, and that if he had lived he would have opposed the Nationalist drive towards authoritarianism. He would certainly have resisted the Draconian legislation which has conferred such exorbitant powers on the executive authority. But what effective resistance could he have offered to a Government which has no scruples about using the unfettered powers of Parliament to entrench itself in office, reduce the Opposition to impotence and turn Parliament into an automatic device to register its arbitrary decisions? Unfortunately, when he made his eloquent and persuasive appeal to the National Convention to trust the people and to trust the wisdom of the future generations he did not foresee that political power could pass into less trustworthy hands than his own – yes, even into the hands of his political adversaries – and that faith in their wisdom could be no substitute for constitutional safeguards. Speaking of Smuts's role in the making of the Constitution, Hancock says 'More than any other national constitution within the Commonwealth, that of the Union of South Africa bears the imprint of one man's mind.' [49] As Smuts was chiefly responsible for making the Constitution, he must bear a proportionate share of the blame for placing an omnipotent Parliament in the hands of the reactionary forces who found it a perfect instrument for their purpose.

NOTES

1. A terraced verandah in front of the house.
2. The People.
3. The term Native is used because it was current at the time. The term African is now in general use. The official term is Bantu, which, however, is incorrect as it means people and is therefore inapplicable to the individual.
4. Black danger.
5. One who comes from, or belongs to, the Cape.
6. Both Sir Edgar Walton and F. S. Malan were members of the Cape delegation to the National Convention.
7. The Protectorates were then known as Basutoland, Swaziland and Bechuanaland.
8. There were three entrenched clauses in the Constitution: Section 35 which protected the Cape non-racial franchise, Section 137 which placed the two official languages, English and Afrikaans, on a footing of equality, and Section 152 in terms of which none of these three sections could be repealed or amended save by a two-thirds majority of the Members of both Houses of Parliament sitting together.
9. Its official title was the Separate Representation of Voters Bill.

Section Two

The Reluctant Deputy

'Our deepest thoughts and emotions are but responses to stimuli which come to us not from an alien, but from an essentially friendly and kindred universe.'

J. C. Smuts, Presidential address to the British Association for the Advancement of Science

I

In 1933, after languishing in Opposition for eight years, Smuts was back in office but not in power.

Once again he was Deputy Prime Minister, but this time he was subordinate to General Hertzog, a man of very different calibre from Botha. Smuts's association with Botha was highly congenial, it was in the nature of a partnership rather than a relationship in which Smuts played the role of subordinate. Smuts was now deputy to a man whose bitter hostility he had endured for more than twenty years. To accept office under Hertzog required of Smuts a profound psychological readjustment such as even politicians, however pliable and accommodating, are seldom capable of making. Hertzog, a man of distinguished charm and courtesy in his personal relations, was the stuff of which zealots are made. As the founder of the Nationalist Party, he was single-minded in his devotion to the cause of Afrikaner Nationalism. It was his tenacity of purpose rather than his intellectual qualities, which were not of a high order, that gained him his ascendancy as *volksleier*[1] and earned him the devotion of his followers. He was a member of the first Union Cabinet, but from the beginning he was at variance with Botha and Smuts on their policy of conciliation.

In his view, the policy of conciliation, which Botha and Smuts treated as a moral obligation after the grant of self-government, compelled them to support Imperial interests and do the work of consolidation for the conqueror. Whilst Botha and Smuts were conscious of the debt of honour they owed to the British for the grants of self-government, Hertzog regarded these acts of the Liberal Government as no more than acts of redress – the British were simply fulfilling their part of the compact of Vereeniging. Conciliation, to Hertzog, meant politically a surrender to the dominant British section and culturally a surrender to the dominant English language. At last Hertzog's open repudiation of the policy of conciliation came to a head in 1912; Botha and Smuts were convinced that Hertzog's activities were reopening the wounds they had devoted themselves to healing, and they dropped him from the Cabinet.

Hertzog immediately became the acknowledged champion of those Afrikaners who were determined to fight for their language, traditions and institutions until, in these things, they attained a status of equality with the English-speaking section. He formulated what he called the 'two-stream policy', according to which Afrikaners and English must develop separately, each in their own cultural sphere, without mixing. At the birth of the National Party the cultural became integrated with the political movement. In 1914 Hertzog accused Botha and Smuts of dragging South Africa, in support of Britain, into a European war with which she had no concern; his attitude, in fact, contributed very largely to a Boer rebellion which Botha and Smuts promptly put down. In 1919 Hertzog led a Boer delegation to the Versailles Peace Conference to plead for the restoration of the independence of the Transvaal and Orange Free State. Botha and Smuts were affronted; they were immensely proud of their achievement in securing separate representation for South Africa at the Peace Conference, and it was indeed a great achievement;

the fact that they were accorded a place at the Conference table as South Africa's official delegates constituted a *de facto* recognition of South Africa's independent status. They naturally resented Hertzog's appearance upon the scene at Versailles as an unwarranted intrusion; they were now convinced that Hertzog was a menace and was undermining their efforts to build a united nation, dedicated to common ideals and bound together by a common love of South Africa.

Smuts, who succeeded Botha as Prime Minister in 1919, became Hertzog's arch-enemy. To Hertzog, Smuts was the lackey of British Imperialism who was intent on betraying his people by leading them along the path of conciliation and delivering them into the hands of his Imperial masters. Smuts was invaluable to Hertzog; no antagonist was better fitted than Smuts to draw his fire, rouse his indignation and serve as the target for his invective. No two men could have been more dissimilar in outlook, temperament, style and even appearance. Their occasional courtesies to each other were no more than perfunctory concessions to convention. They were bitter antagonists, not play actors who assail each other before an audience and who can then have a friendly chat or exchange a few pleasantries behind the scenes. The antagonism between Hertzog and Smuts – vehement and vindictive on the part of the former, cold and contemptuous on the part of the latter – had become an ineluctable fact of political life, a legendary feature of the political scene. It became the nodal point of the political struggle, made a personal drama of every issue, sharpened every controversy, and was of immense importance to the electorate, who decided their attitude to any issue not in accordance with its intrinsic merits but in accordance with their allegiance to the contending champions. Yet it was under Hertzog that Smuts accepted office in a coalition Government. How had this extraordinary conjuncture, quite unpredictable and seemingly impossible, come about?

II

Life is complex and politics is unpredictable; and political life, by a process of synergism, is more complex and unpredictable than both combined. Even while the antagonism between Hertzog and Smuts dominated the political scene, there was a strong undercurrent in favour of reunion – a growing desire to heal the breach which had begun with Hertzog's quarrel with Botha and Smuts in 1912 over their policy of conciliation and which now divided Afrikanerdom into two hostile camps. There was a strong feeling that the time had come to put an end to all racial strife and discord and, above all, to end the political feud which penetrated almost every Afrikaner home, sundered families, turned son against father and brother against brother in bitter enmity.

And strangely enough, whilst there was no sign of any abatement in the antagonism between Hertzog and Smuts, there was in fact, in terms of policy, a convergence between them. This convergence owed much to a more flexible attitude on the part of Hertzog who was becoming less isolationist in outlook. He could now claim – and no doubt felt it was a tribute to the success of his rule – that the Afrikaans language was firmly established, that it had attained an unassailable position and that the Afrikaner need no longer fear that his culture would be submerged by a dominant English culture. Culturally, Briton and Boer were now on a footing of equality. And politically, too, he could claim to have advanced the cause of South Africa's independence. He had returned from the Imperial Conference in 1926 in triumph – the Balfour Declaration, defining the new British Commonwealth of Nations, had recognised the sovereign independent status of South Africa. On his return home, receiving a hero's welcome, he declared that secession from the Commonwealth would give them no more freedom than they possessed already:

'It would not be in our interests; it would be foolish and I believe that if it were proposed not 5 per cent of the population could be got to vote for it.' [1]

In point of fact the Balfour Declaration did not lay the foundations of the British Commonwealth of Nations; it registered certain relationships which had already evolved and which it was convenient and desirable to put on formal record.[2] And to the evolution of the Commonwealth Botha

and Smuts had made a considerable contribution; they had in fact gained *de facto* recognition for South Africa's independent status when they had insisted that South Africa was entitled, in its own right, to representation at the Versailles Peace Conference. Hertzog, of course, gave no credit to either Botha or Smuts for the part they had played in securing an enhanced status for South Africa. What mattered, however, is that Hertzog's attitude had undergone a profound change.
is that Hertzog's attitude had undergone a profound change:

'There was no longer a single reason, Hertzog declared in 1930, why South Africans belonging to the two cultures should not feel and act together in the spirit of a consolidated South African nation.' [2]

He now saw Anglo-Afrikaner co-operation as essential to the welfare and progress of South Africa. In a word, Hertzog was ready to return to the policy of conciliation which he had repudiated in 1912. The two streams could now flow into one broad channel.

Foremost amongst those who sought to advance the cause of reunion was J. H. Hofmeyr. Still a young man in politics, Hofmeyr was a wonder-child whose progress had been marked by a remarkable precocity at every stage of his career. He had matriculated when the milk of the feeding bottle was hardly dry on his lips. At the age of 15 he graduated B.A. with first-class Honours, attaining first place in the examinations. He went to Oxford, as a Rhodes scholar, under the care of a possessive mother, and passed first class in Honours Moderations, with 12 distinctions out of 13 possibles. At the age of 22 he was appointed Professor of Classics and at 24 became Principal of the University College of the Witwatersrand. These were but the first steps in a remarkable career which was cut short when he died at the comparatively early age of 55, still tied to his mother's apron-strings, the aura of a wonder-child clinging to him to the last.

When Hofmeyr attained the age of 29, Smuts appointed him Administrator of the Transvaal. When Smuts was reproached for elevating so young and inexperienced a man to such high office, he reminded his critics that he himself was even younger when Kruger appointed him State Attorney of the Transvaal – and the choice had not been without merit.

As Administrator, Hofmeyr was an outstanding success. Stocky, dishevelled, not impeccably vestured and not over-scrupulous in his ablutions, he was an unprepossessing figure; but when he blinked at you behind his spectacles, you were immediately aware of an alert, extremely orderly and logical mind, with a prehensile grasp of the matter in hand, however complicated it might be. He handled the Provincial budget with a superb mastery which presaged a future Minister of Finance. His public appearances on the platform were highly impressive; his oratory, classical in style, was distinguished not so much for eloquence or verbal felicities as for its incisive logic and economy of phrasing. Here, it was confidently predicted, was South Africa's man of destiny – a future Prime Minister. Towards the end of his term of office as Administrator both the major political parties made a bid for his allegiance. Smuts confidently expected that the young man whom he had honoured would join the South African Party; Smuts, indeed, let it be known that he contemplated retiring from politics – he was now in his 59th year – and would like to groom Hofmeyr as his successor. Hertzog made it clear, through emissaries, that Hofmeyr would receive a warm welcome in the Nationalist Party. Hofmeyr, however, would not declare his intentions. He maintained an enigmatic silence, keeping both parties in suspense, not in order to enhance his scarcity-value – he was not that kind of politician – but because it seemed to him that neither of the Parties could satisfy his immediate aspirations. At last, however, he revealed his mind. On Union Day, 1928, he broadcast an earnest appeal for reunion: he urged 'the coming together of the two larger parties in South Africa, and the formation of a great new party of all those who have the same general outlook'. Hofmeyr's speech caused a stir; it reflected the mood of the electorate and of a substantial number in both political camps. But it led to no action; it set nothing in motion, and there was no attempt, either spontaneous or organised, to fulfil the dream. He personally made no attempt to mobilise his support and fashion it into an effective instrument of action. Eventually he decided to throw in his lot with Smuts.

He fought a by-election and achieved a handsome victory over his opponent. He was promptly received into the hierarchy of the Party and assured of high office on Smuts's return to power.

Smuts had been in Opposition for four years when Hofmeyr joined him. Smuts was not happy out of office; he did not take kindly to the role of leader of the Opposition. To sit on the Opposition benches was a new experience to him. In politics he had gone straight to the top. He did not have to fight his way upwards from the back-benches to executive office. He did not have to make his mark in Opposition. From the first, he had become accustomed to a position of authority, indeed to a dominant position, in the affairs of state. Purposeful activity – to do, to plan, to command – had formed the texture of his daily life. To criticise what others were doing, to oppose their designs without being able to take matters into his own hands for more effective handling, all that was an irksome business. Moreover Parliament kept him occupied for no more than six months in the year. Most dedicated politicians would have occupied the interval between Parliamentary Sessions in planning their strategy for a return to power. But not Smuts. He relied on little more than his personal prestige to ensure his ultimate return to power. In the meantime he turned to study and meditation, and beguiled the tedium of political life out of office by developing certain philosophical ideas on which he had brooded intermittently since his Cambridge days. The result of his ruminations was his book *Holism and Evolution,* a work which he completed in eight months.

Holism and Evolution tells us more about Smuts than about the Universe. It partakes, therefore, more of revelation than of philosophy. In brief, it tells us what system Smuts would follow if he, Smuts, were the cosmic driving force. In his scheme of things, the evolutionary process, operating as a continuing creative force, produces wholes in an ascending order of perfection. For, in his view, each completed whole acquires a special significance by virtue of its wholeness. The whole therefore transcends the sum of its parts; and the parts have no viable reality as parts, and are meaningful only as they are related to the whole and contribute to the value of the whole. This hypothesis would acquire validity if it could be established that the Deity, in his conduct of cosmic affairs, sought the same holistic goals as Smuts – but this has yet to be demonstrated.

It became an intriguing exercise, especially on the part of his political opponents, to interpret Smuts's political aims in the light of his holistic philosophy. Both critics and admirers shared the view that his enthusiasm for Union, for the Commonwealth, and for the League of Nations was inspired by the belief that they fulfilled his holistic conceptions on the temporal level – they represented bigger and better wholes. But actually, in his vision of the future, there was no grand design, embracing all the elements of a multi-racial society, and resolving its discords in a new and viable synthesis. In the field of race relations he offered no solution based on the holistic view that a multi-racial society is actually enriched by the contributions of its various racial groups, creating a diversity in unity. Even when he was intent upon the making of a perfect Union – his first holistic enterprise – he introduced a dichotomy into the process; he insisted that White unity must come first, leaving the Native question to be settled at a later stage, thus relegating to the future an unresolved issue which could conceivably have a disruptive effect on the Union he sought to establish as a permanent structure. In short, Smuts could assign no meaningful role to the Native in his philosophical system – the Native, it appears, simply fell by the wayside as the cosmic process advanced towards its holistic goals.

Thus in the field of practical politics, his philosophy gave him neither guidance nor inspiration. The absence of an effective Native policy in his planning lost him a crucial election in 1929. In his bid for power he could offer no alternative to Government policy. True, an Opposition need not necessarily offer an alternative. It could offer a substitute. It could adopt an attitude of 'me-tooism'. It could say, in effect, 'We shall do what the Government is doing – but we shall do it better. We shall substitute efficiency for ineptitude.' In the United States, for example, the Opposition usually makes this claim. But Smuts could offer neither an alternative nor a substitute. He could offer no alternative because he, too, stood for White supremacy. He could offer no substitute because he could not convince the electorate that his method of enforcing White supremacy would be more effective than Hertzog's. In brief, Smuts, because he could offer neither an alternative nor a substitute, stood before the electorate with empty hands. If his return to power had depended upon his finding an effective answer to Hertzog's challenge on the Native question – the dominant issue in South African politics – he would have languished in Opposition long enough to add several more volumes of philosophic speculation to his *Holism and Evolution*, all equally remote from the actual problems which, as a practical man of affairs, he had to face. Luckily for him, a crisis, a sequence of events, unforeseen and, as far as he was concerned, entirely fortuitous, brought about a change in his fortunes.

III

In 1931 the world was in the grip of the Great Depression. Britain made a desperate effort to maintain the value of the pound sterling. She even formed a National Government to ensure that 'the pound would look the dollar in the face'. But it was all in vain. Within a few weeks of the formation of the National Government, Britain was forced off the gold standard and the pound was devalued.

This shattering event had widespread repercussions, not least of all in South Africa, which had close economic and financial ties with Britain. Moreover, South Africa was the source of half the annual supply of gold to the world. In terms of sterling, the price of gold had risen by 36 shillings per ounce.[3] Could South Africa resist the temptation to follow sterling and thus ensure an immediate rise in the price of her principal product? Were there sound reasons for remaining on the gold standard and renouncing the apparent benefits of devaluation? These were questions of momentous importance.

Smuts was in England at the time. He had been invited to preside over the Centenary meeting of the British Association for the Advancement of Science – an honour which he described as the greatest in his life. The moment the British Government went off the gold standard he was aware that the implications for South Africa were immense. He immediately consulted leading economists – including probably Maynard Keynes who was a close friend of his ever since they worked together at the Versailles Peace Conference – and on the strength of their advice sent urgent cables to South Africa to follow sterling without delay.

The Nationalist Government reacted immediately. The mere fact that Smuts, whose actions were always suspect in Nationalist eyes, urged that South Africa should follow the example of England, aroused resentment. To go off the gold standard was not simply an economic issue to be decided on its merits. It became a burning political issue. The Government regarded it as a challenge to their spirit of independence. Here was an opportunity to demonstrate that South Africa was no longer tied to Britain's apron-strings – she was mistress of her own household. To cling to the gold standard was an assertion of her sovereignty in the economic as well as the political sphere. Hertzog pledged his Government to remain firmly on the gold standard – his Government would resign rather than yield on this issue.

As a matter of fact, in the early stages of the gold standard controversy, the Government received strong support for its firm stand. Seven leading economists issued a statement in support of the Government's decision, arguing on orthodox lines that leaving the gold standard would set an inflationary spiral in motion which would swiftly annul the illusionary benefits that would flow from the increased price of gold. In fact Smuts's own party was inclined to agree with the Government. Hofmeyr objected to the devaluation of the currency on ethical grounds – presumably he believed that it was equivalent to the practice of 'clipping the coinage' initiated by King John. And even the powerful Chamber of Mines was at this stage strongly averse to a departure from the gold standard as the subsequent and inevitable rise in working costs would reduce the profits on gold production to their previous level.

The opposition to the course Smuts urged upon the country was therefore formidable. Yet Smuts's advice was sound. Gold was the foundation of South Africa's prosperity. The gold mining industry required very special consideration. Anything that could prolong the life of the mines would confer a corresponding benefit on the country. The mines were referred to rather loosely as rich mines and poor mines according to the grade of ore mined; but they were rich or poor only in relation to each other. Generally speaking, although the gold fields were extensive, the ore was of a low grade, lying close to the margin of payability. Indeed, a number of mines were barely profitable and vast quantities of ore in every mine could not be exploited because the grade, at the current price of gold, was too low. An increase in the price of gold would transform the whole situation. It would give the whole industry a new and highly profitable lease of life. It would increase the tonnage of available ore. Vast quantities of accessible ore would come within the zone of payability. Rich mines would become richer; dying mines would be rejuvenated; entirely new goldfields would be opened up. An increase in the price of gold would mean not only a prosperous gold-mining industry; it would mean a great accretion of wealth to the country as a whole. The 'golden multiplier' would have a widespread effect; it would produce a wave of prosperity which would flood the whole country. As far as South Africa was concerned an increase in the price of gold would, like the wave of a magic wand, put an immediate end to the depression.

When Smuts returned to South Africa he found the country 'strangled in a noose of gold'. He immediately started a campaign against the gold standard. The Chamber of Mines, which at first was opposed to leaving the gold standard, now supported him. The Chamber of Mines was in fact an embarrassing ally; in the eyes of the Nationalists, the Chamber was the symbol of the capitalist money-power which had been the root cause of South Africa's troubles in the past, from the Jameson Raid onwards. The 'alliance' between Smuts and the Chamber of Mines served only to strengthen the Government's resistance to the attack on the gold standard.

In Parliament the issue was debated for twelve consecutive days. The personal attacks on Smuts were savage. Hertzog in particular was unsparing in his tirades; he was called to order by the Speaker no less than four times. He stole the thunder of his backbenchers, excelling the most vituperative of them in his invective against Smuts. 'We shall stand by this policy,' he declared. 'We will adhere to it while this House, as has hitherto been the case, supports us in this policy.'

Havenga, the Minister of Finance, however, was in serious trouble – he could not make ends meet. He introduced a budget which showed a deficit of two hundred thousand pounds – an enormous deficit by the standards of those days. Smuts, very cleverly, by way of contrast, produced a budget based on the effects of following sterling; his budget, allowing for increased benefits to both civil servants and taxpayers, showed a surplus of £750,000. Revenue from the gold mines alone, as a result of the enhanced price of gold, would fill the treasury to overflowing!

Smuts's budget was received with open derision on the Government benches and with a muffled incredulity, a muted scepticism by his own followers – it belonged to the realm of fantasy! But actually his budget proved to be an underestimate of the benefits which accrued to the country when eventually it did go off the gold standard.

Whilst the gold standard controversy raged unabated, the depression deepened. The Provincial Council of the Orange Free State could not pay the salaries of its schoolteachers – it was, in effect, bankrupt. The plight of the farming community was especially grim – they could not sell their produce in overseas markets. They certainly could not compete with Australia, whose wool and fruit found a ready market in England because the Australian currency was devalued to an even lower level than sterling. The Government offered subsidies to the struggling farmers but these were of little avail. For the situation was aggravated by a drought, the worst drought within living memory, a phenomenon which was interpreted by the pious Boers as a sign that the Government, because of its mismanagement of the country's affairs, had forfeited the Divine favour.

The conviction began to spread that Hertzog's course was run. Smuts, campaigning in the country, felt that the tide was now running strongly in his favour. An early election would assure him of victory. His premonition was fully confirmed when Strauss, his former private secretary, won a by-election by a spectacular majority.

But the Government had dug itself in – it ignored all the signs. It clung even more obdurately to the gold standard. Both farmers and townsmen, in their despair, prayed for salvation – would it come before the Government plunged the country into irretrievable disaster?

A saviour was at hand. Tielman Roos, recently retired from the Cabinet because of ill-health, was now a Judge of the Appeal Court in Bloemfontein. The tranquillity of the Bench was not very congenial to him. His health was improving but boredom supervened. He loved the political arena. He was a shrewd tactician, and was in fact the architect of victory in the elections of 1924 and 1929. Genial, gregarious, indolent, he loved nothing better than to sit in his favourite corner in Turkstras – a cafe noted for the excellence of its coffee where much political history was made – and entertain his circle of friends with sardonic comments at the expense of his colleagues and opponents, chiefly at the expense of his colleagues. People amused him. Politics amused him. Intrigue amused him most of all. A group of dissident Nationalist M.P.s, in their despair, turned to Tielman Roos. The situation called for his intervention. He was the only man who could save the country from ruin. They besought him to return to politics. Neither by temperament nor inclination was he cast for a Messianic role, but when the call came to save the country he could not resist the opportunity to bring off a spectacular political coup as the crowning achievement of his career. He announced his resignation from the Bench and called for a National Government whose aims, he declared, must be to take the country off the gold standard and to end the bitter racial strife which had brought the country to the verge of ruin. In a word, he offered a 'new deal' for South Africa.

The effect of his return to politics was dramatic. His meetings drew excited crowds. He received standing ovations from massed audiences in every big centre, beginning with an overflow meeting in the Johannesburg City Hall. His journey from Johannesburg to Cape Town was a triumphal progress. At every stop a group of farmers gathered about his coach to wring his hands in gratitude, to hail him as their saviour and cheer him on his way. What gave force to his appeal was not that his appeal was more eloquent and incisive than that of Smuts – it appeared that, unlike Smuts, he was in a position to do something about it! He was in a position to force an immediate change of government. He had a secret list of some fifteen M.P.s who, at a signal from him, would cross the floor of the House and bring down the Government.

It now appeared that the fall of the Government was imminent. Events gathered a momentum of their own and moved faster than Tielman Roos had anticipated. The Stock Exchange, which had been in the doldrums ever since the onset of the depression, literally exploded into a boom, the most spectacular in its history. There was a wild scramble for gold-mining shares; novices who had never before touched a share were suddenly enriched. There was a constant run on the banks; people were drawing money and sending it to London, certain of bringing it back at a handsome premium when the country went off gold. The drain of funds compelled the banks to make an urgent appeal to the Government. The Government had to act quickly. It put an immediate stop to all exchange transactions. From that moment the country was virtually off the gold standard. On the following day, the Government made a formal announcement to that effect.

Thus was South Africa forced off the gold standard. But, despite its pledge that it would stand or fall by the gold standard, the Government made no move to resign. Hertzog even found a scapegoat – the capitalist money power had forced the hand of the Government. It therefore had no intention of resigning; it had promised that it would never voluntarily leave the gold standard; the fact that it had been forced to do so absolved it of any obligation to resign – the sort of casuistry which only a politician could offer without a blush.

Tielman Roos went on campaigning. He wanted a National Government not only to take the country off gold – this he had now accomplished – but to bring about reunion. His call for a National Government was of course an invitation to Smuts to join forces with him. He began negotiations with Hofmeyr and eventually saw Smuts himself. He offered Smuts an equal number of seats in a Cabinet of ten; he, Roos, was to be Prime Minister. He could not concede the Premiership to Smuts because his supporters would not serve under a government which was not headed by a Nationalist Prime Minister. He was firm on this point – ' you could not swing a dog into the movement from the Nationalist ranks unless there is to be a Nationalist Prime Minister' he had told Hofmeyr. [3] He told Smuts that he understood his difficulties 'but what would be his, Roos's, standing if he succeeded in doing no more than bring over true Nationalists to Smuts?'[4] On further questioning, it appeared that his Parliamentary support was not as firm as he had at first claimed. He still has his secret list of fifteen M.P.s but it emerged that their allegiance to him was not unqualified. They would support Roos only if he succeeded in forming a coalition with Smuts and were thus assured of not losing their seats. The truth of the matter was that now that the Government had gone off gold, Roos's bargaining power was greatly diminished. He had shot his bolt. His position now depended upon the success of his negotiations with Smuts.

Smuts was obviously not prepared to safeguard Roos's future at the expense of his own. Smuts, however, had to face his caucus; M.P.s and Senators were restive; they could not understand why he was so reluctant to come to terms with Roos. Victory, they felt, was within their reach; a deal with Roos would place it within their grasp. Smuts was asked to summon a caucus. He faced a highly critical body of M.P.s and Senators. They argued for three days. But Smuts declared emphatically that he would never do a deal with Roos. He argued, in effect, that the issue was no longer the gold standard; the issue now was reunion. A bargain with Roos might lead to the fall of the Government; it might bring victory but it would not serve the cause of reunion. Roos would no longer be seen in the light of a saviour of his country. A deal with Roos and his handful of dissident M.P.s – who would no doubt be branded as traitors by Hertzog and his loyalists – would, if it achieved its object, thrust the bulk of the Nationalist Afrikaners into the wilderness. This would only perpetuate, indeed exacerbate, the strife and bitterness which it was the aim of reunion to resolve. By the end of the debate, Smuts had firmly re-established his authority over the caucus. It was resolved that matters be left entirely in his hands.

Smuts, however, was placed in a very unhappy situation. Although the outcome of the caucus seemed highly satisfactory, apparently giving him a free hand, he had, in fact, very little room for manoeuvre. Events had forced him into a situation where he had to make himself a champion of reunion. Having deprived the caucus of victory, he had to do something decisive about reunion; having rejected Roos, he had no alternative but to make an approach to Hertzog. Yet for Smuts to make an approach to Hertzog seemed, even at that stage, impossible and even inconceivable. But no other course was open to him.

The day following the caucus debate, Smuts rose in the House and made his first approach towards a reconciliation with Hertzog; he offered to join Hertzog in the formation of a National Government. His offer was sufficiently explicit in its terms to satisfy the requirements of the situation. In making the offer, however, he could not refrain from chiding the Government for not honouring its pledge to resign when it went off the gold standard. As Leader of the Opposition it was undoubtedly his duty to do so; he could not condone a breach of the constitutional proprieties on the part of the Government. But, having decided to make a gesture in the cause of reconciliation, it was hardly the moment to choose for administering a stern rebuke to Hertzog. It invited retaliation. And that possibly is what Smuts intended, hoping, perhaps subconsciously, to provoke Hertzog into a rejection of his offer.

Hertzog reacted to Smuts's speech with a fury which exceeded anything that Smuts could have anticipated. Vehemently he repelled the accusation that he had broken a pledge. Smuts, he asserted, was guilty of falsehood and distortion in his statements about the Government's commitment to the gold standard. The Government had pledged itself to a firm stand against 'a voluntary departure from the gold standard, i.e. a departure without being compelled to do so by economic facts'. The Government's concern now was to protect the innocent sections of the public 'against the self-interest and rapacity of those persons who already have much to thank the action and assistance of the Leader of the Opposition . . . for the enforced quitting of the gold standard'. Hertzog rejected Smuts's offer to participate in a National Government with bitter contempt:

'Let us assume that all this coalition business is honestly meant and that it is not merely a political fraud. Suppose then that all the three parties with all their various principles and in spite of all their mutually conflicting interests, ideas, aims and religious beliefs were to embrace one another within the same coalition or National Government Kraal what do you think would be left of that Kraal at the end of the first session of Parliament? . . . No, along the way of coalition there is nothing to be obtained for the people of South Africa, at any rate for that section that are honest and honourable. On the other hand, for the disappointed ones, the job-seekers and those who cherished grievances there is everything to hope because in such circumstances there is always something that drops as pickings. We are seeking for an opportunity for bettering the racial relationships, not how to supply carrion for the vultures . . .' [5]

After Hertzog's torrent of invective, it was clear that reunion was dead – killed stone-dead. Smuts, however, despite his gruesome experience at the hands of Hertzog, could view the situation with a sense of relief. He had done what had to be done. He had made his offer – more could not be expected of him. He was free. He had, no doubt, the inner tranquillity and contentment of a man who had done his duty. He decided on an excursion to the top of Table Mountain. Smuts loved to climb the mountain. It was a ritual rather than an exercise. It kept him spiritually as well as physically fit. All mundane cares would drop from him as he ascended the heights. When at last he stood on the summit, he experienced his moment of exaltation. Leaning on his tall stick, he could contemplate as far as the distant horizon – and with the eye of the spirit even beyond – the splendours of his friendly and kindred universe.

Smuts, however, had reckoned without the zeal of young Hofmeyr. This young man now saw an opportunity to bring about the reunion which he had appealed for at the threshold of his political career. He had important contacts in the Hertzog camp. He had made himself a go-between – a role which, in the cause of reunion, he embraced with alacrity and discharged with enthusiasm. Whilst Smuts was 'up on the mountain' surveying the universe *sub specie aeternitatis*, Hofmeyr was busy with his contacts, notably with Pen Wessels, a close confidant of Hertzog.

On his descent from the mountain, Smuts found Hofmeyr waiting for him in his study. Smuts's mood of philosophic serenity was quickly shattered – Hofmeyr was the bearer of incredible tidings. He had a message. Hertzog wanted Smuts to renew his offer; he would indeed welcome a second approach from Smuts. The effect of the incredible news on Smuts was traumatic. How indeed could Smuts forget his recent experience in the House? He had made an offer to Hertzog – it was treated with contumely. In making this approach he had exposed himself to a virulent attack, probably the worst in the long history of his exchanges with Hertzog. Smuts had become inured to Hertzog's tirades. Usually he sat unperturbed – apparently Sphinx-like and impassive – under the rain of insults which descended upon his head. But this time it was different. He had made an offer to Hertzog – extended the hand of friendship – and it was spurned. Deep within him there was a feeling of bitter resentment at the contemptuous treatment he had received from the vindictive Hertzog. How could he serve under such a man? To renew the offer would be to abase himself – to kiss the rod. Hofmeyr, deeply moved, watched Smuts struggling with his pride, the steely blue eyes looking into the distance, the nervous fingers drumming on the desk. Hofmeyr waited in silence. At last Smuts came up with a suggestion. 'Let them have a National Government by all means. He would give it his blessing; he would support it, but he would not accept office in it.' Hofmeyr indicated quite clearly that the suggestion was void of merit. After all, it was Smuts who had called for a National Government. He was personally committed to it. Moreover, his chief lieutenants, Deneys Reitz and Patrick Duncan, would feel deserted and would certainly not enter a National Government from which Smuts stood aloof. A personal reconciliation between Smuts and Hertzog was a pre-condition of reunion. Only the close co-operation of the two leaders could ensure its success.

For Smuts there was no escape from the situation – largely of his own making. Smuts in his pride faced a cruel dilemma. He could retreat, but not without loss of honour; he could renew his offer, but not without loss of dignity. On 1 February Smuts faced his Canossa. He stood up in the House and renewed his offer. He began on a penitent note. 'Perhaps I am to blame,' he said, 'perhaps I handled the matter unskilfully. I did not mean to start a dog-fight.'[6] Having scattered the ashes over his head, he renewed his appeal for National unity. He was ready to serve in a National Government under Hertzog.

There was no immediate response by Hertzog. He, in his turn, had to face a caucus of his party. He told his followers that he could not allow Smuts's appeal to go unanswered. He confided to caucus his belief that the Nationalists would lose the next election.

Hertzog was immediately opposed by Dr Malan. Hertzog's prediction that the Nationalist Party would lose the next election was strongly repudiated by Malan. He denounced it as defeatism, unworthy of the leader of the Nationalist Party. What Hertzog proposed, said Malan, was a union of parties. It was not a true reunion; it was not what was meant by '*hereniging*'[4]. *Hereniging*, as he understood it, was a 'bringing together of those who by inner conviction belonged together'. It could by its very nature embrace only true Afrikaners. No doubt there were individual Afrikaners in Smuts's party, the South African Party, who were worth saving and could therefore be admitted to the fold. But how could they unite with a party which consisted largely of English-speaking elements who had no real affinity with the Afrikaner and who would never share his aims and aspirations? Moreover, misguided Afrikaners like Smuts, who believed in a broad South Africanism in which such English-speaking elements had a rightful share, must be treated as renegades. Thus the intransigent Malan, preaching a narrow and exclusive Afrikaner Nationalism, fought strenuously to prevent a reconciliation between Hertzog and Smuts. From that moment began the rift between Hertzog and Malan which, in due course, developed into a deep schism and resulted eventually in the formation of the Purified Nationalist Party.

In view of the division of opinion in his caucus Hertzog decided to take matters into his own hands. He was prepared to lose support, perhaps as many as twenty or thirty members of his caucus, as the price he must pay for a coalition with Smuts – a coalition which would ensure his remaining in power. On 14 February he sent coalition proposals to Smuts.

IV

Why was Hertzog so intent upon remaining in power, even at the cost of splitting his own party? Politicians, generally speaking, find it easier to renounce their principles than to abjure the seats of power. But if Hertzog sought to retain office, it was not for personal or opportunistic reasons. Hertzog had a deep sense of mission, derived from the historic past. It governed his whole conduct in public life.

Ever since the Great Trek, the Afrikaners saw history in terms of an epic struggle for freedom and survival. To win their freedom they had ventured far from British rule and faced the unknown perils of the Kaffir lands to the north. To ensure their survival they had to master and subjugate the Kaffir hordes. In travail, and at last in triumph, they had set up their independent Republics. Their purpose was fulfilled, for the Republics were to them bastions of freedom, buttressed with laws which guaranteed White survival.

But the struggle was not yet over. British might had struck down their Republics. British rule, from which they had sought escape, had once more overtaken them. Even their survival as a White race was threatened by British rule under whose aegis liberal institutions had been established in the Cape and might now be extended to the North.

Hertzog stood four-square in the Voortrekker tradition. He saw his task as a continuation of the Afrikaner struggle for freedom and survival. History had imposed a twofold obligation upon him. To regain what had been lost in the Boer War and to perpetuate White supremacy as the only method of ensuring White survival.

Half his task had been accomplished. The 1926 Imperial Conference recognised and confirmed South Africa's claim to sovereign independence. He returned in triumph from that historic conference to announce that Dominion status satisfied the aspirations of the Afrikaners for independence and that secession from the Commonwealth could not give them more freedom than they already possessed.

The other half of his historic task had still to be accomplished. Hertzog, with characteristic tenacity of purpose, was determined to bring about a final settlement of the Native problem, a settlement which was to be the crowning achievement of his career as a statesman. It would represent a final solution in that it would entrench White supremacy and ensure a safe future for White South Africa – the complete triumph of the Voortrekker spirit. The chief obstacle to his ambitions was the Cape Native franchise: to ensure that White supremacy would hold sway over the whole of South Africa this formidable obstacle would have to be removed.

In 1926, during his first term of office, Hertzog had introduced in the House of Assembly a Native Representation Bill which provided for the abolition of the Cape Native franchise and for the representation of the Natives throughout the Union by seven White M.P.s, to be elected on a separate or communal roll. This Bill, however, was not proceeded with in the House and in 1927 was referred to a Select Committee. In 1929 the Select Committee produced a new Bill in terms of which (1) the Natives in the four Provinces would immediately elect two Senators, and two more Senators at the end of ten years, and (2) Natives in the Cape already registered as voters were to retain their franchise but no more Natives were to be admitted to the common roll; new voters were to be placed on a separate or communal roll and, as their number grew, they could gradually elect more Parliamentary representatives up to a maximum of two Senators and three M.P.s, all these Parliamentary representatives to be White. Hertzog introduced this Bill in a Joint Sitting of the two Houses. It was, however, opposed by the South African Party led by Smuts; Hertzog therefore failed to obtain the two-thirds majority required in terms of the entrenched clauses to secure the enactment of the measure.

In the 1929 general election Hertzog reaffirmed his determination to achieve a final solution of the Native problem and made the abolition of the Cape Native franchise a major issue in the election capaign. True to his promise, he followed up his victory by producing two Native Bills which, taken together, constituted his 'final settlement'. The pivotal measure was the Bill to abolish the Cape Native franchise. The second measure, a Bill designed to facilitate territorial segregation, provided for the purchase of 15,000,000 acres of land to be added to the existing reserves which were approximately 22,000,000 acres in extent. Despite his electoral triumph, Hertzog still did not command the two-thirds majority required by the Constitution to abolish the Native representation. He used the device of a Joint Select Committee of the two Houses in an effort to secure a sufficient measure of agreement between the Government and the Opposition to ensure the passage of his Bills in a Joint Sitting. The deliberations of the Joint Select Committee revealed that there were a number of Opposition members, notably the Natal contingent, who shared Hertzog's views on White supremacy and in principle were not at all averse to supporting his aims. Smuts, however, in the Joint Select Committee, steadfastly opposed the proposal to abolish the Cape Native franchise, and it was evident to Hertzog that Smuts's opposition to the Bill would deny him the two-thirds majority which would be necessary to make it law. Hertzog, thwarted in his designs, had to reconcile himself to the fact that there was very little prospect of his Native Bills reaching the Statute Book.

Now suddenly an unexpected opportunity presented itself to Hertzog. A coalition would create an entirely new situation.

It would virtually assure him of the necessary two-thirds majority he required to realise his dream. The opportunity had to be embraced!

Smuts and Hertzog met to negotiate the terms of the Coalition agreement. The question of South Africa's status within the Commonwealth presented no difficulty. Hertzog was satisfied that the Imperial Conference of 1926 had conferred sovereign independence upon South Africa; and his declaration that secession could not bring them more freedom than they already possessed had allayed the fears of the English-speaking section – their ties with Britain would not be severed. True, there remained the vexed question of the divisibility of the Crown. When the King of England was at war, could he in his capacity as King of South Africa remain neutral? Would a declaration of neutrality not in fact be an act of secession from the Commonwealth? This issue was capable of arousing the passions of both English and Afrikaners. Smuts's English-speaking supporters would insist that if Britain was at war they could not leave Britain to fight alone. Hertzog's supporters however would insist that association with Britain did not oblige them to go to war for her sake. Smuts and Hertzog, however, decided that the question was only of academic importance. The horizon was unclouded by any threat of war; the League of Nations had been brought into existence to eliminate the causes of war and to keep the peace; the Kellogg Pact, outlawing war, had recently been signed. Both Hertzog and Smuts deemed it expedient to be silent on an issue which time and perpetual peace were bound to resolve.

It was when the two leaders gave their attention to the Native question that the negotiations ran into serious trouble. Hertzog decided that he must embrace his opportunity on the very threshold of coalition. Accordingly he demanded that Smuts should agree that his proposals in regard to the Cape Native franchise should be written into the terms of coalition. This presented Smuts with an insuperable difficulty. In principle Smuts was probably not averse to a change in the Cape non-racial franchise. At the National Convention, whilst he had agreed that the Cape should retain its non-racial franchise laws, he was not in favour of entrenching them and urged that they should be alterable by a bare majority. Clearly he did not regard the political rights of the Natives as inviolable. In 1929 he had opposed Hertzog's Native Representation Bill largely because some of his Parliamentary supporters in the Cape would lose their seats if the Native voters were removed from the common roll. What did concern him now was that his reputation was at stake. At this stage of his career he had become a world figure of great distinction, widely celebrated as a champion of freedom, as an upholder of rights. How could he associate himself with or even countenance any measure to despoil the Cape Natives of their political rights – the meagre but precious political rights of a largely voiceless people? Smuts knew that in the vicissitudes of public life, the transition from pedestal to pillory can be very swift. From the heights he had attained, Smuts was not prepared to contemplate such a sharp descent.

Smuts called Duncan and Hofmeyr into consultation and told them that the negotiations were on the verge of breaking down. He had tried to persuade Hertzog not to make an agreement on his Native Bills a condition-precedent to Coalition, but without success. Duncan and Hofmeyr suggested that an alternative course would be to enter into coalition and thereafter treat the Hertzog Bills as non-party measures, subject to the free vote of the House. Smuts, however, would not accept their suggestion. By such an arrangement he might secure a free hand for those of his followers who could not subscribe to Hertzog's proposals in regard to the Native franchise, but he himself would be committed, otherwise the agreement would in fact be no agreement. Smuts's own standpoint was that no decision on the Bills should be taken at this stage or incorporated in the agreement, but should be left for consideration by the two parties in coalition. It was virtually the same formula he had urged at the time of the National Convention – 'Let us have unity first and settle the Native problem afterwards.'

Hertzog could see that Smuts was very unhappy. Very wisely from his own point of view he decided that it was best to avoid a breakdown in the negotiations. If the attempt at coalition failed, his own chance of securing the passage of his Native

Bills, especially the highly contentious Bill to alter the Cape non-racial franchise, would vanish. Hertzog was astute enough to realise that he could afford to give way without surrendering the advantage he would derive from a coalition. He knew that a number of S.A.P. members shared his views on White supremacy and, under a coalition government, free from their former party allegiance, they would not hesitate to support his measures. As he assessed the situation, the fact that he had failed to secure an agreement on the threshold would not seriously diminish his prospects of securing the necessary two-thirds majority at the appropriate time – an assessment which was to prove correct.

At their next meeting, Hertzog was most conciliatory; he diffused his ineffable charm over the proceedings and was content to obtain from Smuts no more than an agreement to make an 'earnest effort' to arrive at a satisfactory solution of the Native question along lines which, without depriving the Native of his right of development, would recognise as paramount the essentials of European civilisation. On 28 February Hertzog announced in the House 'that agreement had been reached to establish a Coalition Government on a basis more or less of equal participation and on the basis of principles laid down before-hand'. Hertzog and Smuts shook hands. The impossible had happened. A historic feud had ended. The two great leaders were reconciled. Smuts took office as Deputy Prime Minister and Minister of Justice under Hertzog in the Coalition Cabinet.

For Hertzog, coalition was a triumph. It was a great and timely rescue operation. His fortunes were at a low ebb – he was heading straight for defeat, a just retribution for bringing the country to the verge of ruin. Coalition restored him to power; it gave him the victory which an election would have denied him. Moreover, it gave him his heart's desire – an opportunity to secure the enactment of his Native Bills. Smuts was to pay an exorbitant price for the privilege of sustaining Hertzog in office as the head of a coalition government.

If coalition was a triumph for Hertzog, it was a setback, if not a defeat, for Smuts. Power had been within his reach; but a sequence of events, set in motion by the intervention of

Tielman Roos, compelled him to renounce victory in favour of reunion. Smuts, however, had his reward. His reluctant acquiescence in a coalition arrangement, in which he was reduced to a subordinate role, was represented as a great and selfless act of statesmanship. In the prevailing enthusiasm for reunion he received great acclaim for renouncing his personal ambitions for the good of the country. It was generally conceded that in consenting to serve under General Hertzog he had made a great personal sacrifice. Two letters, of the many he received, were typical and reflected the general attitude towards Smuts:

The Governor-General, the Earl of Clarendon, wrote:

> 'But what I particularly want to say to you now is how much I feel South Africa owes you . . . In spite of the general expectation of the success of yourself and your party at the next general election you put aside all personal and party advantages in favour of a step which, in your view, was in the best interests of the Union. This self-effacing act on your part has, I am confident, earned you the affectionate esteem and unbounded admiration of one and all . . . this very grand thing you have done is a deed which will gloriously enrich the pages of South African political history.' [7]

The other letter was from the widow of President Steyn. She decided that the time had come to end the long estrangement which had subsisted between the Steyns and the Smuts family. She wrote, 'If an angel from Heaven had told me last January that this would happen I would not have believed it . . . Never did I think you would be willing to serve under Hertzog. I honour and admire your great courage and sacrifice.' [8]

Smuts made a virtue of necessity: he was soon persuaded that to make a success of reunion was to be his lifework.

In the case of Tielman Roos the spirit of irony was less subtle. He was now the forgotten man. He, the harbinger of reunion, was excluded from its embrace. His success in forcing the Government off the gold standard had rendered his services unnecessary. He had been the perfect catalyst – he had brought about change without experiencing any change in his own condition. His health failed and eighteen months later he died in penury. A number of friends, who, having advance information of his intention to leave the bench, were able to enrich themselves by timely operations on the stock market, acknowledged their debt of gratitude to him by attending his funeral.

V

Prior to an immediate election, a Cabinet was formed, Hertzog as Prime Minister choosing five ministers and Smuts as Deputy-Prime Minister choosing an equal number of ministers.

Malan refused to serve in the cabinet. He issued a manifesto, supported by twenty-nine of his followers, censuring the conduct of Hertzog in forming the coalition. Hertzog, he stated, had acted on his own in beginning negotiations with Smuts and had entered into coalition without consulting either his Cabinet or his caucus. Hertzog's promise of a final settlement of the Native problem was no more than an attempt to make coalition palatable to his Nationalist followers.

After this manifesto it should have been apparent to the political leaders that the rift between Hertzog and Malan was now irreparable. But in view of the impending election, Malan decided upon a piece of political opportunism as bare-faced as it was successful. Malan knew that neither he nor his faithful band of schismatics stood much chance of being re-elected if they broke with Hertzog at this stage and rejected coalition. Very astutely, therefore, Malan and his followers decided to fight the election under the coalition banner to make sure of regaining their seats before making a final break with Hertzog. The result of the election showed how sound their judgement was: of those who refused to endorse coalition only two Roosites, two Natal Home Rulers, and two Labourites won their seats. Pirow, one of Hertzog's loyal lieutenants, denounced Malan and his followers 'for creeping back to Parliament under a banner which was not their own'. But Malan was less to blame for practising the imposture than Hertzog for conniving at it. Hertzog behaved irresolutely in allowing the dissidents to enjoy the protection of his banner. He should have forced them out of his camp and compelled them to fight under their own colours. Smuts was equally lacking in foresight. When Malan was in serious trouble in Calvinia, which looked like rejecting him, Smuts rushed to his rescue, appeared on his platform and saved him from certain defeat. Between them, Hertzog and Smuts lost their one chance of destroying Malan, who eventually triumphed over both Hertzog and Smuts, destroying the former and defeating the latter.

The general election proved that the feeling of the country was overwhelmingly in favour of reunion; and it was followed by a strong movement towards ensuring the permanence of reunion by merging the two parties into one. 'Fusion' was the popular term for the merger. What gave further impetus to the demand for fusion was the fact that under the Coalition Government the economy was making a rapid recovery and was in fact forging ahead – a fertilising stream of wealth was flowing from the gold mines, making the whole country prosperous. And the rural areas too were experiencing the benefits of reunion – the drought had broken and the country blossomed as never before after the abundant rains – clearly a sign that the Divine blessing had descended upon the country and the Government had been restored to grace.

The movement in favour of fusion gathered momentum. Hertzog came out openly for fusion. Smuts, who was overseas at the time, attending the World Economic Conference, returned home to find his party executive in the Transvaal already committed to it. He wrote:

'The fact is that in the rural Transvaal the urge towards fusion is very great and the Executive probably had its hand forced. I shall see that there is proper consultation and co-operation between all sections of the Party. But of course I agree and believe fully that in the end there is likely to be fusion. Dr Malan and his stalwarts may soon split off, and that too may ease the position for many S.A.P.s.' [9]

Smuts was right about Malan, but the process by which Malan was 'to split off and ease the position of the S.A.P.s' was to prove far more painful for Smuts than he anticipated. The trouble began when Hertzog put his plan for the fusion of the Parties before the Cape Congress of the National Party; of the 172 delegates present 142 voted against the proposal. A week later at Bloemfontein, at the meeting of the federal council of the party, Hertzog fared much better – he carried the other three provinces with him. The Cape, however, decided to stay out of fusion. This was a serious blow to Hertzog. He was ready to reconcile himself to the loss of Malan but he could not afford to lose the Cape.

Malan, however, made a final effort to resolve his differences with Hertzog. He visited Hertzog at *Groote Schuur*[5] for what he described as 'openhearted talks'. There followed a series of exchanges which afford a perfect example of how the political game is played by two superb tacticians, matching their skill against each other. Malan knew that in pursuing the constitutional issues he was entering upon the area of disagreement between Hertzog and Smuts – a highly sensitive area. Relentlessly, with clinical precision, he probed the tenderest spots in that area. Ostensibly seeking reassurances, Malan touched each delicate spot in turn. Could South Africa secede from the Commonwealth? Could South Africa declare itself neutral in the event of war? Was Hertzog prepared to appoint a South African as the next Governor-General? Was Hertzog prepared to abolish appeal to the Privy Council and make the Supreme Court in Bloemfontein the final court of appeal?

Hertzog apparently gave satisfactory answers to all these questions, stating in particular that he never doubted South Africa's right to neutrality and secession. Malan, of course, was not interested in reassurances for their own sake. His aim was to disrupt the negotiations between Hertzog and Smuts, to put an end to fusion, and to restore the old party divisions. If he did not succeed in putting an end to fusion, he would at least turn it into a fusion between a reunited Nationalist Party and that section of the South African Party which was prepared to accept the Hertzog–Malan interpretation of the Constitution, leaving Smuts with a diminished following consisting largely of the English-speaking section who could never identify themselves with Nationalist aspirations. Malan came within an ace of succeeding. He issued a statement in which he paid tribute to Hertzog for making every effort to reach agreement on matters of vital importance, and he endorsed Hertzog's appeal to Nationalists to end the quarrel. Smuts was deeply affronted. It appeared to him that the terms of fusion were being settled between Hertzog and Malan, and that he, Smuts, was being brushed aside as if the matter was no concern of his. Smuts decided to write a letter to Hertzog to inform him that he was no longer prepared to negotiate fusion. The letter was actually delivered to *Groote Schuur* with an intimation that a copy would be handed to the press. However, on the following day, Smuts, yielding to the entreaties of his colleagues, withdrew the letter and apologised to Hertzog for being so maladroit as to write it.

Hertzog and Smuts resumed their negotiations. When Hertzog and Smuts had discussed the terms of coalition the negotiations had run into difficulties over the Native question; in discussing the terms of fusion, their negotiations once again ran into difficulties – this time their main task was to resolve their differences over the constitutional issues. It was not only because of Malan's studied persistence in raising thorny questions such as the right of secession and the right of neutrality that the negotiations proved difficult. These issues did indeed embarrass Smuts because they caused anxiety and even alarm amongst his English supporters; they were in constant fear that fusion would call for concessions which would erode their deeply cherished association with the Commonwealth. Smuts had won the confidence of the English-speaking section ever since the days when Botha and he had initiated their policy of conciliation; they looked to him as their trusted champion to preserve the links which bound South Africa to the Commonwealth. But it was not only his concern for the sentiments of the English-speaking section which made him resist any attempt to sever or weaken the Commonwealth ties. Basically the negotiations ran into difficulties because Hertzog and Smuts were irreconcilably divided over the question of South Africa's role and destiny within the Commonwealth.

Hertzog's standpoint – the Nationalist standpoint – was

that the interests of South Africa must at all times, whether in war or peace, take precedence over those of the Empire. After the Imperial Conference of 1926, and the Statute of Westminster which gave legal force to the Balfour Declaration, he was content to remain within the Commonwealth, because, as he declared at the time, secession could not confer greater freedom on South Africa than she already enjoyed, and on that understanding Anglo-Afrikaner co-operation was assured. In other words, although a Republican at heart, he was prepared to accept the Commonwealth connection – provided it did not impair South Africa's autonomy or restrict her freedom of action – because it served to allay the fears of the English-speaking section and thus promoted good relations between the two language-groups.

Smuts, on the other hand, had a far more positive attitude to the Commonwealth and a broader appreciation of its value to South Africa. Perhaps because of his holistic philosophy, he believed in the future of the Commonwealth and he believed that South Africa gained in significance by being associated with the Commonwealth as a larger whole. To the Commonwealth South Africa owed in a large measure her security and economic well-being. To occupy an important place in a great and powerful community of nations undoubtedly enhanced the national prestige. As a member of the Commonwealth, South Africa could be an effective force – her statesmen could help to shape and influence Commonwealth policy in relation to world affairs. No one understood this more clearly than Smuts himself, for the part he played in the councils of the Commonwealth both in war and peace had made him a statesman of world renown, thus enhancing not merely his own reputation but – what was more important – the prestige of his country.

Of course Nationalist politicians like Hertzog and Malan shared neither his vision nor his aspirations; they recognised no call to greatness. To them the Commonwealth was merely the British Empire under another name. In point of fact, as Smuts knew, the British Empire as an aggressive force had ceased to exist. It was no longer predatory and overbearing. It had outlived its epoch of expansionism. It was in fact coming to an end by a process which was giving new freedom and vitality to an existing structure. This process of de-imperialisation was unique. Hitherto empires, in their decline, have either disintegrated or, more usually, have fallen a prey to some rival imperialism. But here for the first time, an empire was coming to an end by a process which was transforming it into a Commonwealth, a process to which South Africa under the leadership of Botha, Smuts and Hertzog had made a great and decisive contribution. This process was complete as far as South Africa and the other dominions were concerned – their autonomy was guaranteed; in due course the colonial dependencies, emerging from a state of tutelage, would achieve their emancipation. The fact that South Africa could play an important role in this process was surely a powerful argument for South Africa continuing its association with the Commonwealth and entering wholeheartedly into its councils. There was no reason at all why the Commonwealth should not undergo a further process of evolution and decentralisation. As Smuts saw it, the next stage in the development of the Commonwealth was a sort of regionalism whereby each Dominion would assume responsibility for the progress and welfare of its more backward neighbours in the colonial empire. South Africa, for example, could take the Protectorates under her wing, and assume responsibility for their development. Then the Dominions would achieve equality of function as well as equality of status. As far as the question of secession and neutrality were concerned, could South Africa be in and out of the Commonwealth at the same time? Could South Africa enjoy the privileges of membership without accepting its obligations? Even if in theory the right of secession were conceded, would not honour and self-interest dictate that South Africa should co-operate with the other members of the Commonwealth and take a full share in its privileges and responsibilities?

It was a noble dream. In interpreting Smuts's attitude to the Commonwealth, it must be conceded that his vision of the future was far too sanguine. He could not foresee that, amongst other things, South Africa would be forced out of the Commonwealth, not because her sovereign status was threatened or imperilled, but because her racial policies, designed to preserve South Africa as a stronghold of White supremacy, would make her unacceptable to the emergent African states destined to play an important – even a preponderant – role in the councils of the Commonwealth. But in the circumstances of the time the argument for Commonwealth co-operation lacked neither force nor validity; it could kindle enthusiasm and fire the imagination. Certainly Smuts's faith in the destiny of the Commonwealth was a sufficient guarantee that in negotiating the terms of fusion he would not leave the English-speaking section in the lurch.

Accordingly, in these negotiations he made it clear, in writing,

> 'that whilst Hertzog personally interpreted South Africa's status as including the divisibility of the crown, the right of neutrality and the right of secession, that was not his own interpretation. He understood that he and Hertzog agreed to differ on these matters and, in consequence, no pronouncement upon them need be written into the new party's programme of principles.' [10]

This statement was accepted by Hertzog. They had found a method not of resolving their differences but of avoiding an open conflict of opinion which might render fusion impossible.

On 5 June the principles of fusion were published and were ready for submission to the parties for their approval. In the northern provinces Hertzog had no difficulty; he carried the Nationalist Party with him. In the Cape, however, he met with a severe setback; Malan defeated Hertzog's motion by 142 votes to 30. In October, Malan and his supporters repudiated Hertzog and in December they formed the Purified Nationalist Party. History had repeated itself. Malan broke with Hertzog as Hertzog had broken with Botha in 1912. According to Malan, Hertzog had renounced his life work and forfeited his claim to the leadership of Afrikanerdom. The mantle had fallen on Malan. As the new *volksleier*, Malan, together with his faithful remnant, would renew the struggle. There would be no more back-sliding and no more betrayals; they would not swerve from their path until their goal was reached. Malan would lead his people to the promised land – an independent Afrikaner republic.

The departure of Malan from the fold eased the situation for Smuts. He had in fact intimated to Hertzog that the S.A.P. would never consider fusion with Malan and his group. Smuts however had his own dissidents to contend with. To appease the republicans amongst Hertzog's followers, Smuts had accepted a proposal that the following article be included in the Programme of Principles:

'While the Party stands for the maintenance of the present constitutional position, no one will be denied the right to express his individual opinion about or advocate his honest conviction in connection with any change of our form of government.'

Smuts thought this a small price to pay for fusion; but Colonel Stallard and six other English-speaking M.P.s rejected it with great indignation; in their view it negated what the S.A.P. stood for; it would open the door to the beginnings of a republican movement which could end in the dissolution of their Commonwealth ties. Colonel Stallard, a courtly old Tory, who would have graced the English scene in the days of Sir Roger de Coverley, led his six followers out of the S.A.P. and formed the Dominion Party.

Thus Hertzog, having shed Malan and his followers on the one hand, and Smuts, having shed Stallard and his followers on the other, joined forces to form the United Party.

Although the Native question – very surprisingly – had presented no obstacle in the negotiations for fusion, it was deemed necessary to meet the scruples of the Cape members and others who had shown some concern about the future of the Cape Native franchise. Article 6 (b) under Native Policy was designed to meet these scruples:

'It is recognised that a solution of the political aspect of this question on the basis of separate representation of Europeans and Natives or otherwise, being fundamental in character and not having hitherto been a matter of party division, should as far as possible be sought through agreement, and should be left to the free exercise of the discretion of individual members representing the Party in Parliament.'

This article, which allowed members the freedom to vote according to their conscience, satisfied the Cape members and others, like Hofmeyr, in the S.A.P.

There was, however, another group to whom fusion was unwelcome. The Native voters on the common roll were not unaware of what fusion had in store for them. Their fears were not groundless.

VI

The fusion of the two parties was now accomplished. The stage was set for Hertzog's assault on the Cape non-racial franchise. His measure – the Representation of Natives Bill – aimed at the removal of all Black voters from the common roll. It not only sought to remove an existing right. Its aim was far-reaching. Hertzog wanted a radical change in the political structure of the country. His measure was designed to dismantle completely the structure of equality which had been firmly established in the Cape for over a century, and to ensure that White supremacy, reinstated in the Cape, would hold uniform and unchallengeable sway over the whole country, from the Cape to its northern boundaries.

Smuts faced a grim dilemma. 'The Natives', he wrote in December 1934, 'are getting more and more suspicious and they think that fusion means they are now without champions and that the Nationalist viewpoint has won.' [11]

Clearly the Natives had looked upon the S.A.P., and particularly Smuts, as the protector of Native rights and interests. Smuts, whatever his motives, had steadfastly resisted any attempt to despoil them of their political rights. In 1929 it was Smuts who had prevented Hertzog from securing the two-thirds majority which would have enabled him to abolish the Native franchise. In 1933 it was Smuts who nearly brought the coalition negotiations to an end because he would not consent in advance to the abolition of the Cape Native franchise; he had refused to be a party to a 'sell-out'. On the strength of this record the Natives were entitled to expect Smuts to act with some degree of consistency in the defence of their rights. How could he abandon them to the fate which Hertzog had in store for them?

Unfortunately, as the result of fusion, Hertzog's authority, as compared with that of Smuts, was immensely strengthened. He was now calling the tune. He knew that there had been a great deal of latent support for his Bill in the old S.A.P.; this support would certainly manifest itself more openly and gain in strength under the banner of fusion. Smuts in all his political career never faced a more crucial issue. As the leader of the S.A.P. wing of fusion his role was of pivotal importance. His attitude to the Bill would determine its fate. Although a substantial number of his followers, especially from Natal, were in favour of the Bill, his authority was not so diminished that he could not count on the support of a sufficient number to deprive Hertzog of the necessary two-thirds majority. If he opposed the measure they would follow his lead and thus defeat Hertzog's attempt at a final settlement.

When Hertzog presented his Representation of Natives Bill to Parliament, it provoked a storm of protest, especially in the Cape. An All-Africa Convention under the Presidency of Professor Jabavu condemned the measure. Sir James Rose-Innes presided over an immense protest meeting at the City Hall in Cape Town. Hertzog, fearing that these mass protests, gathering in volume, might have a decisive influence upon the Cape M.P.s and deprive him of their support, decided to modify the Bill. The Cape Native franchise was to continue but all Native voters would be placed on a separate or communal roll and would have the right to elect three White representatives to Parliament. Hertzog could afford to make this concession. To place the Native voters on a separate roll and give them a limited number of White representatives would serve his purpose equally well. For a separate roll was no more than a device – a highly effective device – for turning a racial group into a permanent political minority and reducing them to political impotence. It was a device therefore to ensure that political power would remain in White hands – which of course accords with the very definition of White supremacy. Smuts immediately declared that the new Bill, which also made provision for the setting up of a Native Representative Council, together with the Native Trust and Land Bill, constituted a *quid pro quo* for the removal of the Natives from the common roll. In view of this, he would support the new Bill.

Hofmeyr, however, was not so easily satisfied. In his view, the Bill which Smuts was so ready to accept as a compromise was even more illiberal than the measure which Smuts and the S.A.P. had opposed in the joint sitting in 1929. Hofmeyr made it his business to see Hertzog and inform him that he intended to oppose the Bill. Hertzog received him courteously, acknowledged his right to oppose the measure on grounds of conscience and told him that he would not call for his resignation from the Cabinet. The interview, as far as Hofmeyr was concerned, was entirely satisfactory.

Hofmeyr's subsequent interview with Smuts was a less happy experience. He informed Smuts that he would not only vote against the Bill but speak against it. Smuts made no attempt to remonstrate with Hofmeyr or dissuade him from his course of action. Smuts, however, according to Hofmeyr's own account 'was very much disturbed'.

The interview was disturbing for Hofmeyr as well. For some time he had an unhappy premonition that he would find himself opposed to Smuts on the question of the Native franchise. In 1935 he had written to Mrs Millin about Smuts:

'. . . his dilatoriness – the tendency to let things develop . . . He shows a tendency to put off doing things which are a little unpleasant . . . coupled with his dynamic energy he also has today a kind of occasional indolence of mind which makes him tend to shirk issues which . . . seem to him unimportant . . . Last year when he returned from England . . . it was clear that the whole idea of an additional colour bar was hateful to him. And yet I feel in my bones that although he has stood out for the Cape Native franchise so far he will let it go without a struggle next year.' [12]

It was not surprising that Smuts was very much disturbed

when Hofmeyr informed him of his intention to oppose the Bill. For Smuts it was a bitter blow – as unkind as the stab of Brutus was to Caesar. Smuts, the renowned liberal statesman, fresh from his visit to St Andrews University where his Rectorial address on freedom had added lustre to his great reputation, was now confronted by a young man in the role of champion of the oppressed! By accepting the Bill he had placed himself in a position where he had to face Hofmeyr as an adversary! And his facing Hofmeyr on such an issue could lend itself only to one interpretation – he, Smuts, had not only abdicated from an honourable role but had betrayed a trust. His great reputation, which had saved him from a dishonourable surrender to Hertzog in the coalition negotiations, could no longer be vindicated if he supported the Bill.

When the Bill was debated in Parliament, he explained his attitude in terms of abject surrender:

'The Natives of the Cape,' he said, 'in fact all over South Africa, attach the greatest importance to this vote of theirs. They look upon it as almost sacred. They look upon it as settling their status of equal citizenship in this country. It was not an ordinary vested right, it went much deeper, they looked upon this as a symbol of equal citizenship in this country. One can understand how in these circumstances they were profoundly and deeply attached to it . . . '

An Hon. Member interjected 'Then why touch it?'

'I say', said Smuts, 'that as far as I could read the situation, this right was in danger of being taken away by Parliament and the Cape Natives being left completely deprived of it without a proper substitute, and it was in those circumstances that I thought the time had come . . . to help in giving them this separate franchise in place of the old system which was in danger. I have never liked the system of separate representation in itself. I have opposed it on former occasions. I have voted against it both in select committees and in the House . . . Of course I could have died in the last ditch so to say. I could have said "I fight to the bitter end for the Cape Native franchise" but what would have been the result? It would not have been I that died, but the Natives metaphorically speaking.' [13]

Smuts said that he was glad that at last a settlement of the Native question had been reached, not an ideal settlement but containing 'the elements of justice and fair play and fruitfulness for the future'.

Hofmeyr's speech, firmly based on principle, represented in every respect a striking contrast to that of Smuts. The Bill, he insisted, was no more acceptable than its predecessors:

'It is called a compromise, but if we look back to 1926, then from the point of view of the Natives it is the Natives who have done all the giving and none of the taking . . . The central feature [of this Bill] is to give to the Natives an inferior, a qualified citizenship which has the marks of inferiority in clause after clause . . . and which bears the added stigma that whatever may be the advance of the Native in civilisation and education, to all intents and purposes he is limited for all time to three members in a House of 153. That surely is a qualified inferior citizenship.'

He went on to warn the House:

'By this Bill we are sowing the seeds of a far greater political conflict than is being done by anything in existence today . . . the crux of the position is in regard to the educated Native . . . They have been trained on European lines, they have been taught to think and act as Europeans, we may not like it but those are the plain facts. Now what is the political future of these people? This Bill says that even the most educated Native shall never have political equality with even the least educated and the least cultured White or Coloured man. This Bill says to these educated Natives "There is no room for you, you must be driven back upon your own people." But we drive them back in hostility and disgruntlement and do not let us forget that all that this Bill is doing for those educated Natives is to make them the leaders of their own people in dissatisfaction and revolt.'

He dismissed Hertzog's claim that his Bills represented a final settlement. Pointing out that an unreasoning fear, together with the sentiment based on tradition, lay behind the Bill, he said:

'These are the facts that made the Prime Minister recede from the relative liberalism of the Bill of 1926; these are the facts that made the Bill of 1929 worse than the Bill of 1926; and made this Bill again worse than the Bill of 1929. And there is no finality. There is no more finality than there was in 1892 when Sir James Rose-Innes supported the Bill of that date because it might bring finality. The tide of reaction is still flowing forward. I know that those of us who are opposing the tide cannot hope to check it. The puny breastworks that we put up must be swept away but I do believe that the mere putting up of those breastworks is going to accelerate the day when the tide will turn . . . I believe there is also a rising tide of liberalism in South Africa. It is mostly the younger people who are in the forefront of that tide. It is they who are the custodians of the future . . . it is by them that the ultimate issues in connection with this matter will have to be decided.' [14]

By common consent it was Hofmeyr who captured the honours in that historic debate. His speech was, in substance, the speech which Smuts should have made. In its defence of established rights, in its ringing affirmation of liberal values, in its call for courage in the defence of freedom and justice, it was exactly in tune with that great Rectorial address which Smuts had only recently delivered at St Andrew's University. Hancock, commenting on Hofmeyr's 'memorable speech', says, as if it were some sort of vindication of Smuts's attitude, that possibly its most telling point was the one that Smuts himself had made six years before, namely that Hertzog's Bill would produce not a settlement but a new unsettlement. Hancock's comment is in fact a telling exposure of Smuts's inconsistency. Instead of standing by his earlier conviction that Hertzog's Bill would produce a new unsettlement – a point which Hancock regards as a formidable indictment of the measure – Smuts now identified himself with legislation which would produce the mischief he confidently predicted.

Although Hofmeyr's speech was greatly admired, its immediate effect upon the House was limited: against the influence of Smuts added to that of Hertzog even the logic and eloquence of Hofmeyr could not prevail. Only eleven members, six of them from the Cape, joined Hofmeyr in voting against the Bill in the joint session. Hertzog's triumph was virtually complete.

Hofmeyr's speech, however, not only earned him a crown of laurels. It achieved far more. It put fresh heart into the liberal forces. In their moment of despair, when their cause seemed lost and betrayed, Hofmeyr stepped into the breach – the Cape liberal tradition found in him, if not its only, certainly its most fearless and eloquent champion. They were defeated but not dismayed. Hofmeyr had unfurled a banner; under such a leader they could rally their forces; they could fight back and, in the fullness of time, reinforced by the younger generation in whom Hofmeyr had such complete confidence, they would regain what they had lost. Thanks to Hofmeyr's speech they had a sense of euphoria even in defeat. Its immediate effect, especially its inspiring call to youth, may have been salutary, bracing them for a further struggle; but few of them realised, at this stage, what an irreparable defeat the liberal cause had suffered – a defeat which only Smuts could have averted.

Why did Smuts make this fateful surrender? Why, faced with this crucial test, did he betray both in the spirit and the letter the principles he had enunciated in ringing tones, in unmistakable terms in his overseas speeches, which had made him in the eyes of the world the supreme champion of freedom? Why, if he opposed the 1929 Bill ostensibly on grounds of principle, did he support the 1936 Bill on grounds of expediency, explaining his action in terms of utter defeatism?

Alan Paton offers an explanation which places Smuts's action in a more favourable light.

'By now,' says Paton, 'the danger of Hitler was clear, and Smuts saw it, though Hofmeyr often complained that he did not see it clearly enough. There can be no doubt that if Britain had gone to war with Hitler, Smuts would have wanted South Africa to be at Britain's side . . . Smuts was prepared to swallow many things in the hope that the United Party could be held together, until the grave logic of events convinced it, whether it liked it or not, that the country which had once overwhelmed the republics was now the champion of liberty in a time dangerous and grave . . . how else can one explain the total acquiescence, the kind of twilight into which his life seemed to have moved? Was he giving Hertzog his head in National affairs . . . so that he himself could lead when the real crisis came? There seems reason to adopt this view.' [15]

This view of Smuts's behaviour is not only Alan Paton's. There is a widely held view that Smuts was prepared to put up with the humiliations he had to endure in the Hertzog Cabinet because he held steadfastly to the belief that war was inevitable, and that his dominant concern was to avoid a break with Hertzog and thus ensure that at the crucial moment he would be in a position to give an effective lead in favour of joining Britain in the war against Hitler. This view, which has become legendary, owes much to hindsight and very little to actual fact. It will not bear analysis. As Hofmeyr observed, Smuts did not see the menace of Nazism as sufficiently ominous to awaken fears of Nazi aggression. Even after Hitler's reoccupation of the Rhineland in 1936 – at the very time Smuts had committed himself to Hertzog's Native Bills – he actually believed that it was possible to come to terms with Germany and that Hitler was far less dangerous than Mussolini. 'He thought coercion was the right treatment for Mussolini but conciliation the right treatment for Hitler,' says Hancock. 'He thought the Italians should be bludgeoned but that the Germans should be persuaded into peaceable behaviour.' [16] And, says Hancock further on, 'From the point of view of the Commonwealth, he saw a distinction between the Fascist and Nazi dictatorships. Italy the friend of yesterday had become a deadly and dangerous enemy. Germany the deadly enemy of yesterday wanted to be friendly.' [17] In a word, Smuts was all for appeasement and believed in its efficacy.

Hancock, in vindication of Smuts, gives a list of quotations from a number of his speeches in which he took pains to declare his conviction that South Africa would take her stand with Britain and the Commonwealth in the event of war. But these speeches, made after Munich when the writing on the wall was plain for all to see, represent a definite change of outlook and could not possibly explain his conduct in 1936 when he supported the Hertzog legislation. Before Munich he said not a word to indicate that he recognised in Hitlerism a new and sinister phenomenon. There was no Churchillian ring in his speeches. There was no warning note against the looming menace of Nazism; and he did nothing to prepare the public minds for an eventual crusade against the evils of Nazism. He was supposed to be endowed with a prophetic insight into the trend of events, but even as late as the Munich crisis he had not come to the conclusion that war, if not imminent, was inevitable. At the time of Munich, he reassured an anxious journalist in characteristic terms, 'the dogs of war are barking but the angels of peace are on guard'. [18] He actually signed a declaration of neutrality which Hertzog, far more apprehensive about the situation than Smuts, had drawn up for presentation to the Cabinet and which all the Ministers dutifully accepted. And according to an authoritative article in the Round Table, which always received its information from authentic sources, Smuts would have stood by his pledge of neutrality and would have been on the side of Hertzog, Havenga and Pirow if war had actually broken out. [19] The evidence shows conclusively that, at that stage, even the advent of war would not have altered his attitude of acquiescence to Hertzog's policies – he was prepared not only 'to give Hertzog his head in National Affairs' but to allow him to decide the destiny of South Africa in a world at war. What then is left of the legend that Smuts was prepared to play an acquiescent role in the Hertzog Cabinet so as to be in readiness for his moment of destiny?

The explanation for Smuts's behaviour in 1936 is far more simple and direct. He was certainly anxious to keep the United Party from breaking up, but for reasons closely related to his own political fortunes. Confronted with Hertzog's Bill to remove the Natives in the Cape from the common roll, he had to make a fateful decision. Could he afford to break with Hertzog and face the prospect of a return to the political wilderness? As the joint leader of the United Party, Smuts carried a special responsibility; he could not allow himself the freedom of action which Hofmeyr enjoyed. If he, Smuts, had voted against the measure his lead would have been decisive – the effect would have been to thwart Hertzog and split the United Party. The consequences would have been disastrous for Smuts. There was no possibility of restoring the *status quo ante* – Hertzog rejoining Malan to reconstitute the Nationalist Party on the one side, and Smuts reuniting with Stallard to reconstitute the S.A.P. on the other. Events had shaken the political kaleidoscope into an entirely new configuration. By no means all of his wing would have followed him out of the United Party. He would have been back where he was in 1929, but with a diminished following and even less prospect of returning to power.

For he could never have lived down the reproach that he had destroyed Hertzog's settlement without having a settlement of his own to offer, and that for the sake of preserving the Black man's vote he had put an end to the great experiment of fusion, especially at a time when, under its beneficent rule, the country was enjoying unprecedented prosperity. Clearly there was no political future for Smuts outside fusion. Smuts must have reflected on the bitter irony of his situation as compared with that of Hofmeyr – the young man who had worked so assiduously to bring about fusion enjoyed complete freedom of action, whereas he, Smuts, who had gone into fusion with such reluctance, was now its captive! For Smuts there was no escape. Unlike Samson, he dared not bring down the walls of the structure that imprisoned him. Unity had to be preserved whatever the price. And as it was the Black man who had to pay the price, it did not seem too exorbitant.

VII

How did the system of separate representation work in practice?

The three Native Representatives took their place in the House of Assembly in 1938. The Natives were fortunate in their choice of M.P.s, who quickly established themselves in the front rank of Parliamentarians. But it was soon apparent that they constituted an isolated group, an enclave in unfriendly territory. The other Cape M.P.s, no longer answerable to Black voters in their constituencies, immediately divested themselves of all concern for Native interests. The responsibility for representing Native interests fell exclusively upon the three Native M.P.s. It was a heavy burden.

As an isolated minority, receiving no support from the rest of the House for any of their pleas or proposals, they achieved nothing of importance for the people they represented. As for influencing the course of legislation, their efforts were a sustained exercise in frustration. Only a sense of dedication kept them going. As a group, they were too impressive to be ignored, too effective in debate to be treated with indifference. They gained the ear of the House, but it was a resentful ear. They were extremely well briefed in their presentation of the Native case – probably too well briefed, for in their authoritative exposure of the Black man's disabilities there was much to trouble the complacency, if not the conscience, of the House. Every plea for the amelioration of the Black man's lot aroused resentment rather than sympathy. The Native Representatives, it appeared, were putting ideas into the heads of their Black constituents, who would otherwise have been blissfully unaware that they had any grievances. From both sides of the House, but with less restraint on the side of the Opposition, the Native representatives were denounced as irresponsible agitators, as whippers-up of Native unrest, and as fomenters of ill-will between White and Black. It was soon apparent that Parliament was not prepared to tolerate the Native Representatives as long as they persisted in representing the Natives.

VIII

Fusion seemed set upon a prosperous course. But the portents were not entirely favourable. The Dominion Party had won East London in a by-election, an indication that Stallard was gaining ground at the expense of Smuts's wing of the United Party. But what troubled Smuts more was the fact that the

Purified Nationalist Party, which began as a breakaway movement, was emerging as a dangerous force in South African politics. Hertzog, who had already lost control of the Cape, was beginning to lose control of the Free State, his own stronghold.

'The Nationalists', wrote Smuts, 'have restarted the old bitter fight – this time mostly from hatred of Hertzog, who is now fought with the weapons and in the style in which he fought me for so long.' [20]

Hertzog fought back fiercely. On 7 November 1935 he made a three-hour speech to the Head Committee of the Party in the Free State, 'acclaiming South African unity and denouncing its wreckers':

> 'What do we see surrounding us today? Indefatigable, zealous attempts in all directions to provoke national disunity, to awaken irreconcilable aversion and hatred between the races: to prostitute our cultural assets, our language and religion, our history and origins, as hostile instruments of attack, with which to fight, to slander and crush one another.' [21]

This outburst, fired by indignation, showed clearly that Hertzog did not underestimate the forces arrayed against him. Malan, a formidable foe, who knew how to exploit the call of the blood in order to bring straying Afrikaners back to the fold, insisted that the Purified Nationalist Party was the only home for true Afrikaners. A shrewd politician, Malan knew too that he had to adopt a more extreme nationalism to establish a successful rival claim to Afrikaner allegiance – a nationalism so extreme that from his new standpoint he could denounce Hertzog, the father of Afrikaner Nationalism, as a renegade, as a traitor to the cause and an enemy of the *volk*. Thus the gap between Hertzog and Malan widened; the difference between the Nationalism of Hertzog and the Purified Nationalism of Malan became sufficiently clear and definable to produce a bitter antagonism.

The Nationalism of Hertzog was a liberating force. It sought to throw off the yoke of British Imperialism and to establish a broad and independent nationhood which would embrace both the English section and the Afrikaans section on a basis of complete equality. The Purified Nationalism of Malan was not a liberating force. Its aim was domination. It sought a state of affairs which would ensure the undisputed ascendancy of the *ware*[6] Afrikaner in every sphere of the national life and reduce all so-called unnational elements – British, Jews and detribalised Afrikaners who followed Smuts – to the status of second-class citizens. The Republic, the goal of all his aspirations, would be founded on the principle of *'Een land, een volk, een taal'*.[7]

The rise of Hitler gave a powerful impetus to Purified Nationalism. Malan and especially his young intellectuals – the theoreticians of the Party – readily succumbed to Nazi doctrines and they were particularly fascinated by the elaborate Nazi pseudology in regard to race. Ever since Fichte, who exalted the Germanic race, and Hegel, who deified the Prussian state, there have not been wanting philosophers and historians who have so re-written German history as to make it appear that from the earliest times – from the days of the Niebelungen Lieder and the Teutonic Knights – the Germans were destined to be a master-race whose mission it was to bend other nations to their service by the power of the sword. This Herrenvolk doctrine was the soil on which Nazism flourished. Captivated by this doctrine, the Purified Nationalists produced their own version of it. Strydom, a future Prime Minister, put it in a nutshell. 'If we do not accept the Herrenvolk idea how can Whites stay the boss?'

But what particularly impressed the Purified Nationalists was Hitler's use of anti-Semitism as the spearhead of his advance to power. Clearly, anti-Semitism was too effective a weapon to be ignored – it had to be pressed into the service of Purified Nationalism.

In the South African scene, anti-Semitism had to be handled with special skill. The Afrikaners, especially in the rural areas, had established good relations with the Jews. The Boer farmers knew the Jew as the friendly store-keeper who tided them over difficult times, or they saw him in the guise of an itinerant trader, the *'smous'*, who brought his wares to their remote homesteads. Moreover, the Afrikaners, the descendants of the Voortrekkers, had repeated in their own history the story of the Exodus; they had sojourned in the Wilderness, and had gone in search of their promised land; they revered the Bible as the authentic revelation of the Divine Will and sought to govern their daily lives in accordance with the loftiest teachings of the Hebrew Prophets. What was more natural than that they should look upon the Jews – the People of the Book – with a certain respect tinged perhaps with awe? Even the humble *'smous'* who displayed his wares on the farmhouse stoep was received with a kindly courtesy and, in a spirit of genial hospitality, was offered coffee, a meal, and even a night's shelter.

But now the Purified Nationalists were teaching the simple and pious Boers that, being of Nordic stock, they were a master-race, superior even to the chosen people! The synod of the Dutch Reformed Church reinforced the message. It appointed a commission to examine the historic credentials of the Jew, and on the strength of its report, the synod solemnly annulled the Divine decree and announced authoritatively that the Jews were not in fact God's Chosen People. Any manifestation of anti-Semitism could therefore not incur the Divine displeasure. And to enable Afrikaners to observe the Biblical injunction 'Thou shalt love thy neighbour' it became their Christian duty to ensure that their neighbours were Gentiles and not Jews.

The Purified Nationalists decided that the first essential step was to prohibit the entry of Jewish immigrants into the country. At that time South Africa was still a haven of refuge for German Jews seeking escape from Nazi persecution. An agitation was started to close the door to these immigrants. Dr Malan declared that South Africa wanted no more Jews as they were an 'unassimilable element'. He denied that there was a Nazi persecution of the Jews, a rather ironic statement for, in effect, he denied that Hitler had put into practice the sort of discrimination he, Malan, was planning to enforce against the Jews in South Africa. Thus he exonerated Hitler, whilst convicting himself of anti-Semitism.

The anti-Jewish agitation gathered strength and rose to a climax when a German ship, the Stuttgart, especially chartered for the purpose, entered Cape Town harbour with a full complement of Jews from Germany. Dr Verwoerd, at that time a professor at Stellenbosch University, addressed a great mass demonstration and threatened to lead a march on Parliament to give vent to the people's anger and resentment against this unwanted and undesirable influx of Jewish refugees.

Hertzog bowed to the storm. He introduced the Aliens Bill, a measure which, in effect if not in form, closed the door to all Jewish immigrants.

The Jews were dismayed. How could Smuts, of all people, acquiesce in such a measure? They recalled that in 1930, in more tranquil times, he had strongly opposed the Quota Bill, designed to prevent Jews from Eastern Europe entering South Africa as immigrants. Much to the consternation of his own party, which, during his absence overseas, had voted solidly for the measure in the second reading, he had on his return fought it single-handed in the third reading debate. On that memorable occasion he had not been afraid to act boldly as the avowed champion of the Jews. Now he was acquiescing in a measure which would close the door to Jews seeking escape from bitter persecution. Once more, to avoid a break with Hertzog, Smuts had to make a concession to fusion – this time at the expense of the Jews.

The Aliens Bill, however, did not pacify or placate the Purified Nationalists. Anti-Semitism was proving too good a weapon; having achieved so much, they were determined to achieve even more. Malan, having closed the door to 'unassimilable elements' from without, now wanted protection against the 'unassimilable elements' within. 'How are we going to find a living for our children? How are the people to regain their lost ground?' To save South Africa from the enemy within the gates, Malan called for a nordic front of Afrikaans- and English-speaking people.

And following the precepts of their Nazi mentors, the Purified Nationalists made a practice of using the term 'Jewish' as a term of opprobrium to be applied to everything they wished to discredit and destroy. Thus, in preparing the public mind for a new order which would bear the unmistakable features of National Socialism, they denounced the decadence of the existing British-Jewish democratic system. In extolling the merits of authoritarian rule and the one-party state, they spoke with contempt of the British-Jewish Parliamentary system. How the ghost of Simon de Montfort, who was an aggressive anti-Semite in his day, must have resented this aspersion on his handiwork!

It is proof, if such were needed, of the virulent nature of anti-Semitism that it could be used to stir up hatred against the Jews of South Africa who, ever since the early pioneering days, had played an important, even an indispensable role, in the progress and development of the country. Even Malan, when he was Minister of the Interior, had praised them. 'The Jews', he said, 'were an important section of the population and they have fully identified themselves with the community and its people.' Now he was denouncing them as an 'unassimilable element'! In one sense, in the only sense that matters as far as the state was concerned, the Jews had proved themselves a readily assimilable element. They had established firm and intimate associations with the country; they had absorbed its culture, they were part and parcel of its social, economic and political life; they had shared its vicissitudes; its welfare was as much their concern as that of any other section of the community.

In any case, the Jewish leaders contended, loyalty not assimilability was the test of citizenship. Loyalty was a simple, clear-cut concept and by that test they were prepared to stand or fall. They had proved their worth as citizens in peace and war; war, which had imposed the supreme test, had not found them wanting; they had taken up arms because in fighting for South Africa they were fighting for everything they held dear. It was, they contended further, a fundamental principle of every democratic state to permit of a diversity of elements, united by a common bond of loyalty; it was the supreme merit of the democratic state that it did not demand conformity to prescribed norms in matters of culture and creed – unlike the Fascist state which tried to achieve unity by enforcing uniformity. South Africa was a democratic country; freedom and liberty of conscience were its basic tenets. Clearly then in defending their rights and dignities, the Jews were not merely defending their own position; they were fighting to uphold principles which were of vital importance to all who believed in democracy. They refused to narrow the issue to one of anti-Semitism. They insisted that the fight against anti-Semitism was part of the wider struggle against the forces of reaction. They knew that their fate was bound up with the triumph of the progressive forces and that they had to play their part in a united effort to defend the common liberties of all, irrespective of race or colour.

The Jews stated their case with firmness and vigour. It would, however, have been far more effective if it had been stated by Smuts. In the past Smuts had not hesitated to champion the cause of Jewry; indeed a colony had been named after him in Palestine in recognition of his great services to the Zionist cause. But at this critical juncture he was silent; he had nothing to say in defence of the Jews at home who, as fellow-citizens, had a claim on his services. Smuts, the statesman renowned for his breadth of vision, had nothing to say on the wider issue – the fact that the reactionary forces were using anti-Semitism to mobilise support for their evil designs on the democratic system; and that what was at stake, therefore, was not the fate of the Jews, but the fate of democracy, of which both Gentiles and Jews were the beneficiaries. Smuts's silence on this vital issue was not an unstudied silence, nor was it enigmatic. Smuts abdicated his role as 'champion of the Jews' in order to avoid embarrassing Hertzog in his fight against Malan, who was busy telling the country that the Government would take no action against the Jews because Smuts – or Smutsowitz, as Malan chose to call him – would not allow it.

It was Hofmeyr who, from the public platform, warned When Malan moved a resolution calling on Parliament to impose restrictions on the Jews, especially in regard to their admission to any trade, profession or occupation – restrictions which in their operation would have been as vicious as those which the Nuremberg laws imposed on the Jews in Germany – it was Hofmeyr who faced up to Malan.

'Today', said Hofmeyr, 'he comes here as the admitted

leader of the anti-Semitic party in all its intolerance and all its childishness. I am not going to express any surprise at the Leader of the Opposition. We know him. We know him as the leader of the Party who without any shame will exploit any sentiment, who will try to encourage hatred and bitterness against any section of the people if they can get advantage out of it.' [22]

It was Hofmeyr who from the public platiform, warned the country that anti-Semitism was the precursor of dictatorship.

'It was', says Alan Paton, 'a frightening year for South African Jews but many of them took courage from the short, thick-set untidy man, who in spite of an almost unbearable Ministerial burden, was here, there and everywhere championing in that ringing, unwearying voice what he believed to be right.' [23]

And it was to Hofmeyr that Mrs Sarah Gertrude Millin wrote complaining bitterly that Smuts – of whom she was such an ardent admirer – in making judicial appointments, had surrendered to the anti-Semitic campaign and ignored the claims of her husband, a leading member of the Bar, whose merits were indisputable.

Hofmeyr wrote in reply a letter both sympathetic and significant.

'I spoke to Smuts but the only result was to show me how weak he had been in this matter of lying down to anti-Semitism. I am ashamed of the Government of which I am a member. Smuts was just as weak over me, just as ready to let the wicked triumph and the forces of reaction prevail . . .' [24]

IX

Hofmeyr, it appears, had grievances of his own. What precisely was he referring to when he said that Smuts 'was just as weak over me, just as ready to let the wicked triumph . . .'? He was referring to some recent unhappy experiences which finally convinced him that he could no longer rely on Smuts's support for the principles which he, Hofmeyr, deemed to be important.

Fusion was running into difficulties. It was a time of troubles for the Government. In Parliament a game at once serious and sordid was developing between Hertzog's wing of the United Party and the Purified Nationalist Party. Despite Hertzog's final settlement, the field of race relations remained rife with possibilities for eager politicians in search of highly emotional issues. The Purified Nationalists were constantly raising such issues in order to create tension between the two wings of the United Party. And the followers of Hertzog raised these issues in an attempt to forestall and outbid the Purified Nationalists in the appeal to fear and prejudice. It was the kind of politics which both sides really understood, and they indulged in it with professional skill and more than professional zeal – it released in them an almost libidinous excitement! Hofmeyr, perhaps inevitably, found himself in the centre of this vortex.

Two prominent members of the United Party, General Pienaar and Mr J. H. Grobler, gave notice of their intention to introduce private members Bills, the former a Bill to preclude non-White traders from employing White persons, and the latter a Bill to prevent White wives of non-White husbands acquiring property.

Hofmeyr, as Minister of the Interior, in a press statement announced that the Government opposed both Bills and would not allow Parliamentary time for them. Unfortunately he gave the two members an opening. In the statement he added that in 1936 the Government had offered to appoint a Select Committee to consider these matters and the offer still stood.

General Pienaar and Mr Grobler promptly put a motion on the order paper asking the House to refer their Bills to a Select Committee. Hertzog consented to give this private motion priority over Government business. In the debate on the motion for a Select Committee, Dr Malan asked for an assurance that the Bills would be treated as a matter of urgency and would be on the Statute Book before the end of the session. Hofmeyr, replying on behalf of the Government, stated firmly 'I am not prepared to give such a guarantee'.

Whereupon Mr Swart, a frontbencher, one of Malan's chief lieutenants, pressed the matter and demanded a guarantee that the Bills would be dealt with before the end of the Session. Mr Pirow, an alert politician, alive to the political implications of these racial measures, followed the progress of the debate with mounting anxiety. At last, he could contain himself no longer. He passed a note to Hertzog to the effect that he proposed to enter the debate, and, despite what the Minister of the Interior had stated on behalf of the Government, announce that he fully supported the Bills. The situation on the Government benches became tense. Hertzog passed the note to Smuts. On reading it, Smuts gathered up his papers and left the House, either to mark his disapproval of what Pirow proposed to do or to dissociate himself from the whole business. Hertzog thereupon rose in his place and moved the adjournment of the debate – an astonishing and unprecedented procedure in view of the fact that he himself had given priority to the debate!

The Malanites were elated. With the help of Pirow they had created a crisis of dissension in the ranks of the Government. Hertzog summoned an emergency meeting of the Cabinet. Could the crisis be resolved? It seemed that either Pirow or Hofmeyr would have to go. In either event it might mean the break-up of fusion. Pirow insisted that the Government must define its attitude to the Bills, and unless it declared itself in favour of these measures there would be a wholesale defection of Hertzog's followers to the Purified Nationalist Party. Hofmeyr, on the other hand, stated equally firmly that if the Government gave its blessing to these Bills he would be compelled to resign. Hofmeyr fully expected Smuts to support his stand. In order to resolve the crisis Hertzog offered a compromise, which Smuts – more anxious to avoid the break-up of fusion than to vindicate Hofmeyr – decided to support. To satisfy Hofmeyr, Hertzog proposed that the Bills be left to the deliberations of a Select Committee, and to satisfy Pirow he proposed that the report of the Select Committee should be considered before the end of the current session. This compromise was accepted.

The compromise was a short-term solution; it merely postponed the issue. What would the Government do if the Select Committee decided – as was highly probable – in favour of the Bills and advised the Government to take immediate steps to prevent Asians from employing White persons and the wives of non-Whites from acquiring property?

Hofmeyr made up his mind as to his course of action. If the Select Committee reported in favour of the Bills and the Government, accepting its recommendations, decided to sponsor these measures and treat them as Government measures, he would resign. He would, however, agree to a proposal that the Bills be left to the free vote of the House; this procedure would absolve him from personal responsibility and leave him free to vote against the Bills.

Smuts, in a letter to a friend, gave his own view of the situation:

'We have had some difficulty in Parliament and the Cabinet over some Colour Bills introduced by private members of our Party. First it was some Bill against mixed marriages which however has for the moment been sidetracked. Then it was two Bills against Asiatics employing white girls, etc. Hofmeyr took a strong line against the Bills, while I have temporized . . . A select Committee is now enquiring into them . . . These colour questions are more and more trouble, and are partly no doubt exploited by our opponents in order to ferment differences of view in the United Party. [Hofmeyr] is a good liberal with a fine human outlook. Unfortunately he is also somewhat academic and exaggerates things and aspects of no real importance . . . I am doing my best to keep him with us, and to some extent sympathize with his standpoint, without thinking the actual points of difference as important as he does. Politics is the art of the possible and the practicable and one has to give in on small things in order to carry the bigger things.' [25]

This letter is particularly interesting because it casts a revealing light on Smuts's approach to political issues during this period. When Smuts spoke of 'small things' and 'bigger things' he conveyed the impression that he was concerned with the appraisal of things of the same order, differing only in terms of their relative value. But the 'small things' and the 'bigger things' with which he was concerned were not of the same order. The 'bigger things' resolved themselves into one overriding objective – to keep fusion viable at all costs. The 'small things' – the matters which Hofmeyr sought to defend on grounds of principle – must be sacrificed to this objective. It was by the deft use of simple phrases that Smuts succeeded in exalting political expediency above principle, and reducing principle to a subordinate role in the conduct of affairs. When Smuts refused to take a firm stand in support of Hofmeyr he not only betrayed Hofmeyr and the principles which Hofmeyr sought to uphold; he did grievous damage to his own reputation. Smuts was fully aware of the fact that his prestige was waning and that Hofmeyr was supplanting him as the champion of the liberal cause. Some weeks later, Smuts wrote:

'The difficulties with Hofmeyr have been finally overcome, but I fear not without having some aftermath of bitterness for the future. I have stood by him, as he is high principled and very able, and I don't want to leave him out for the future. He is now looked upon as the only liberal in the Cabinet, and I am looked upon with doubt by many. The way of a peace-maker is a hard one, and as it has been my bitter lot for a long time, I don't mind.' [26]

As Smuts's conception of the role of a successful peace-maker obliged him to capitulate to Hertzog on every major issue, his lot could be described as a bitter one in the sense that it earned him very little kudos, and in fact much discredit. As for saying 'I don't mind', the most pertinent comment is that of his biographer. 'But of course', says Hancock, 'he did most intensely mind, partly because he felt that his loyalty towards Hofmeyr had fallen under suspicion, partly because he recognised the instability of fusion – that is to say of his life work.' [27]

X

Smuts would probably have been less troubled about his relationship with Hofmeyr if the acts which brought his loyalty under suspicion had succeeded in their purpose of making fusion a more stable structure. Smuts must have become aware at this stage that his efforts to avoid a break in the United Party and his concessions to Hertzog were weakening his own position without having the effect of strengthening the viability of fusion. His importance in the Cabinet was dwindling; the Prime Minister no longer consulted his Deputy on matters of moment. In fact, Hertzog had reached the stage where he took it for granted that, however high-handed he might be in the conduct of affairs, Smuts would acquiesce in whatever he decided to do.

It was a high-handed action of Hertzog that once again raised tension to the point of crisis in the ranks of the United Party. Without consulting Smuts, Hertzog decided that at the opening of Parliament 'Die Stem', a patriotic Afrikaans song, should be played after 'God Save the King', which had been played at every opening of Parliament since 1910. When the two airs were played at the opening ceremony, Stallard, at the earliest opportunity, rose in the House and put a question to Hertzog – he wanted to know whether 'Die Stem' had now become the National Anthem of South Africa. Hertzog gave a tortuous reply; he said that 'Die Stem' might one day be recognised as the national anthem, but that in fact the Union had no national anthem legally or officially recognised, or generally esteemed as such in the hearts of the people of South Africa.

' " God Save the King",' he said, 'was the National Anthem of Great Britain and the fact that it is still played here, and perhaps looked upon by many of our English-speaking fellow citizens as the National Anthem of the Union, is merely due to our historic past as a subordinate part of Great Britain. And he went on to say that "God Save the King" would continue to be received with respect when played on appropriate occasions, not because it was a South African National Anthem, but because of its "primary and obvious character as a solemn invocation to the Almighty for His protection of our King".'

In reply to a supplementary question by Stallard, Hertzog

went even further – he gave assent to the view that either now or in the process of time 'Die Stem' would displace 'God Save the King' as the national anthem of South Africa.

It was Hertzog's reply even more than the actual playing of 'Die Stem' that precipitated the crisis. Smuts immediately left the House. Blackwell, a United Party front-bencher, went to see Smuts. According to Blackwell's account he found Smuts 'looking white and shaken' and asked him what he was going to do about it. Smuts replied: 'You must leave me out of this. My position with the Prime Minister is much too delicate. Go and see him yourself.' [28] As Smuts had virtually abdicated his responsibility in the matter, Blackwell went to the Chief Whip and told him that it was essential that he, with other leaders of the English-speaking opinion in the House, should have an immediate interview with the Prime Minister. The following morning, Blackwell, at the head of a deputation, waited on Hertzog. The Prime Minister received them with his customary courtesy. Blackwell, 'speaking with respect but with the utmost plainness', told Hertzog that they were gravely shocked by the attitude he had taken up, and that 'it was certain that his attitude would cause a stampede of the English-speaking voters away from the United Party at the forthcoming general election'.

Blackwell offered a compromise. If Hertzog would acknowledge that 'God Save the King' was the national anthem, Blackwell and his colleagues would have no objection to the introduction of 'Die Stem' as a second and local national anthem, giving to it a parity of status with 'God Save the King'. Hertzog, however, refused to compromise – no doubt mindful of a possible stampede of Nationalist voters to Malan. He would never admit that 'God Save the King' was the official national anthem of the Union. But, he added, whatever its status might be, he had no wish, in introducing 'Die Stem' to supplant 'The King'. The introduction of 'Die Stem' would be supplementary to that of 'The King'. Blackwell and his colleagues were satisfied with this statement and ended the interview amicably upon an assurance that in reply to an additional question in the House, Hertzog would make it clear that the introduction of 'Die Stem' would be supplementary to that of 'God Save the King'. And so the crisis was resolved.

'It is an extraordinary thing', says Blackwell, 'that throughout the whole of this incident which threatened to break up fusion, the Prime Minister does not appear to have consulted General Smuts at all.' According to Blackwell, Hertzog did not consult Smuts about the playing of 'Die Stem' at the opening of Parliament.

'I am certain that he did not consult him about his first anthem reply or about the second one given on Monday . . . This was symptomatic of the way the Prime Minister was ignoring him although fusion had been brought about as a working partnership on a fifty-fifty basis between the ex-Nats., led by General Hertzog and the ex-S.A.P.s led by General Smuts, and ever since the Hertzog–Malan split the ex-S.A.P. section of the party was much the stronger.' [29]

Smuts played a passive role in the whole anthem affair. But when the crisis was over, it was he who received the tributes – by his genius for compromise, it was generally said, he had succeeded in keeping the United Party together.

The United Party had once more surmounted a crisis of dissension. But how long could it continue to exist as a viable political force? It had always been assumed that a reconciliation between Smuts and Hertzog would be permanent and would ensure the success of fusion. But was fusion strong enough to resist the disruptive forces that were assailing it on both flanks? It had no inner cohesion: there was no unifying principle to hold it together. The challenge of Malan on the one flank and the challenge of Stallard on the other, were producing corresponding tensions within the United Party, disturbing the relationship between its two wings and impairing its stability. The United Party had to pursue an uncertain course; it could not veer too much to the one side or too much to the other without coming to grief. And as for Smuts, he had clearly made up his mind to keep the United Party together at all costs, even if it meant his making these humiliating surrenders to Hertzog, not because fusion was his 'lifework' but because the only alternative was a return to the wilderness. And, of course, the claim that he was trying to save his 'lifework' could serve as a face-saving pretext for continuing his endeavours.

XI

Smuts had professed a strong desire to keep Hofmeyr in the Cabinet; but it must have been clear to Smuts that, if he continued on his present course and failed to support his 'highly principled and very able' young colleague when he took a stand on principle, a break between them was inevitable. Hofmeyr would part from Smuts with reluctance. He owed Smuts a certain loyalty. After all, it was Hofmeyr who had worked so zealously for fusion; it was his intervention as a go-between at a crucial moment that had led to the reconciliation between Smuts and Hertzog. But it was largely Smuts's fault that he had become disenchanted with fusion and no longer found the United Party a congenial political home. Smuts, as Hofmeyr wrote in his letter to Mrs Millin, was too ready 'to let the wicked triumph and the forces of reaction prevail'. As for being a member of the Cabinet, his saying in the same letter 'I am ashamed of the Government of which I am a member' indicated pretty clearly that he was ready to quit should the occasion arise. The occasion was not far off.

In the general election of 1938, Mr A. P. J. Fourie, Hertzog's Minister of Commerce and Industries, was defeated by the Purified Nationalists. Hertzog, however, decided that he must have Fourie back in his cabinet. Hertzog's loyalty was commendable, but his method of reinstating his colleague in office was reprehensible. In terms of the Constitution the Governor-General, acting on the advice of the Cabinet, had the power to nominate four senators by virtue of their 'thorough acquaintance with the reasonable wants and wishes of the Coloured races'. One of these had resigned and Hertzog decided to take advantage of this provision to get Fourie into the Senate. Fourie had not the slightest claim to the appointment; he had no acquaintance with the reasonable wants and wishes of the Coloured races; yet Hertzog proposed to use this provision in the Constitution as a convenient side-door by which Fourie could gain admission to the Senate. Hertzog's decision was a gross violation of the letter and spirit of the Constitution, a gesture of contempt as far as the Senate was concerned, and an affront to the Coloured people whose interests were of so little concern to Hertzog that a provision in the Constitution which was designed to ensure a respect for their wants and wishes could be used as a convenient side-door by which anyone, irrespective of his merits, could at the whim of the Prime Minister be brought into the Senate.

Hofmeyr refused to be a party to the appointment of Fourie as a Senator. He went to see Hertzog and told him so; he, Hofmeyr, could not agree to the appointment because Fourie did not qualify as a Senator in terms of the Constitution.

Hertzog, however, brushed Hofmeyr's objection aside. At a cabinet meeting, called for the purpose, Hertzog formally appointed Mr Fourie as a Senator. Smuts was not present at the Cabinet meeting, but he made it known that he would support the appointment of Fourie to the Senate. For Hofmeyr the fateful moment had come – he promptly sent in his resignation.

In a tense atmosphere, Hofmeyr rose in the House to defend his action:

'I consider it as nothing less than a prostitution of the Constitution that that provision should be used to assist the Government out of a temporary political difficulty . . . but this issue is not merely a constitutional issue . . . it touches the whole question of the relations between the European and the non-European peoples in South Africa . . . and this issue is simply this . . . are we going to allow the non-Europeans to be made pawns in the White man's political game?'

Hofmeyr went on to say:

'I am not prepared to share responsibility for a breach of the Constitution, and I propose to go . . . I have been told that this issue is not big enough for resignation. Of course for those whose primary concern is political expediency no issue is ever big enough.'

'Mr Speaker', Hofmeyr said in conclusion, 'may I in all

modesty express the hope that this action of mine will be a clarion call to the younger generation of South Africa to set principle above expediency in the approach to public affairs.' [30]

Hofmeyr's resignation from the Cabinet was followed a few days later by the resignation of Claude Sturrock who had declared that he stood by Hofmeyr in opposing a breach of the Constitution. Smuts, however, despite the fact that he had lost two of his best colleagues, did not think the issue big enough to warrant his intervention against Hertzog on their behalf. He made it known that he supported the Prime Minister in this matter because his main concern was to save fusion.

According to Alan Paton, Hofmeyr, in a letter to a friend, expressed the belief 'that if Smuts had taken a stronger line, the Prime Minister would have abandoned his intention to nominate Fourie as a senator . . . but when it became clear that Smuts would not resign, Hertzog grasped the chance to get rid of two troublesome Ministers'. [31]

And in a letter to Sarah Gertrude Millin, Hofmeyr wrote as follows:

'I am sorry for Smuts. He has been sorely humiliated. To a large extent it was his own fault. He is really no match for the Prime Minister in simple directness and in straightforwardness of purpose. He is now Hertzog's prisoner in the Cabinet. He must do whatever he is told. His only possible escape is through the outbreak of war and the almost inevitable Cabinet split which will result. At the moment our relations are somewhat strained; mainly, I think, because, knowing he has let me down badly, he is sensitive about the whole business . . .' [32]

XII

Hofmeyr left the Cabinet but remained a member of the United Party. He was not refused the whip, which meant that he could attend the caucus and take part in its proceedings. Hofmeyr's remaining in the Party meant of course that there was more trouble in store for Hertzog and more humiliation for Smuts. And indeed it was not long before Hofmeyr was seriously at odds with Hertzog, creating yet another crisis in the United Party. Stuttaford, Hofmeyr's successor as Minister of the Interior, introduced the Asiatics (Transvaal Land and Trading) Bill, the purpose of which was to preclude Indians from buying land outside the defined Indian areas. Smuts acquiesced to this measure, and received by telegraph a strong protest from Gandhi: 'Why is agreement of 1914 being violated with you as witness? Is there no help for Indians except to pass through fire?' [33] Hofmeyr was prepared to support the Bill as an interim measure; but as Stuttaford would give him no assurances to that effect he decided that it was an iniquitous measure and that he would oppose it.

The Purified Nationalists of course supported the Bill; Hofmeyr, who was joined by Blackwell, constituted the whole opposition to the measure. Together Hofmeyr and Blackwell put up a splendid fight, opposing the Bill clause by clause and repeatedly dividing the House in committee-stage, without, however, gaining a single point.

This, however, was more than Hertzog could stand. His patience was now exhausted. He was going to brook no more trouble from two such turbulent members of his Party. Hofmeyr was a constant source of trouble because of his liberal convictions, Blackwell because he was always up in arms in defence of the rights and sentiments of the English-speaking section. They were summoned to appear before the caucus. The Prime Minister moved a vote of censure on Hofmeyr and Blackwell. They were unrepentant and said firmly that if the vote of censure was passed they would resign from the caucus. Smuts intervened on behalf of his two colleagues and moved that the caucus express dissent not censure but he pleaded in vain – Hertzog made it clear that the alternative to a vote of censure was his own resignation. 'Smuts', says Hancock, 'submitted to Hertzog's will. Among liberal-minded South Africans, his reputation by now was at its nadir.' [34]

It was, however, to be Smuts's last surrender to Hertzog.

XIII

In Europe the storm clouds were gathering fast. They were dark and ominous. The question now was when would the storm break?

At the time of Munich, the previous year, Smuts was convinced that the crisis would be resolved without recourse to war. He even signed the statement which Hertzog had drawn up and which committed the Government to a policy of neutrality in the event of war between Britain and Germany. Smuts did not see appeasement as Churchill saw it – as a process which strengthened Hitler at the expense of Britain and her allies and, with every concession, reduced their power to resist his mounting ambitions. He did not view Munich as Churchill viewed it – as an abject surrender which would pave the way for further surrenders to Hitler's insatiable demands. Nor did he share the view of Chamberlain's apologists – that Munich secured a much needed respite for Britain, enabling her to build up her military resources for a final confrontation with Hitler at a more propitious hour. When Chamberlain returned from Munich in the incongruous role of Hotspur, claiming that he had 'plucked the flower safely from the nettle danger', Smuts accepted the claim at its face value. He saw it as a genuine success for Chamberlain's diplomacy. 'After Munich', says Hancock, 'he gave credit to Chamberlain. He did this most emphatically in a broadcast address for Armistice Day 1938. The choices last September had seemed stark – nothing but brute force or abject surrender – until Chamberlain's intervention saved the peace and gave the world a second chance.' And, says Hancock, 'he ended his broadcast by considering ways and means of restoring the League and making it even at this late stage, a comprehensive and authoritative guardian of the world's peace'. [35] With Hitler on the rampage, this belated effort to restore the hapless and derelict League of Nations must surely strike one as the height of ingenuousness, quite remarkable in the case of a statesman widely credited with a profound, indeed a prophetic insight into the trend of world events.

It was, however, not long before the inexorable march of events began to convince Smuts that his view of the world situation at the time of Munich had been far too sanguine. 'By early 1939', says Hancock, 'his fears began to predominate over his hopes.' [36] It was high time he gave rein to his fears. The omens were clear and conspicuous; there was no need to search for them in the entrails of a chicken or to gaze deeply into a crystal ball. The rape of Czechoslovakia, Chamberlain's pledge to Poland, the Ribbentrop–Molotov pact of non-aggression – this sequence of events signified beyond doubt that Europe was on the brink of war.

For Smuts the moment of decision was at hand. The question of neutrality was no longer a matter for speculation. It was a live issue. In recent months he had made speeches, alerting the public mind to the gravity of the situation and revealing clearly the direction of his thinking. He denounced neutrality as an impossible dream and urged that in days of danger South Africa must seek for safety in a close co-operation with her friends and associates in the British Commonwealth of Nations. On the outbreak of war there would be a split in the Cabinet on the question of neutrality. He would have to give a decisive lead in favour of participation in a war against Germany. It was the one issue on which he could afford to take a firm stand. It was the one issue on which he could command the loyal support of the whole of his wing of the United Party and could probably rally to his side a majority of the members in the House. It was, therefore, the one issue on which he could triumph over Hertzog and thus return to power.

It is true that he had the previous September, at the time of the Munich crisis, signed a declaration of neutrality, carefully committed to writing by the Prime Minister. Hertzog would no doubt insist that the document represented the settled policy of the Government and was binding on the members of the Cabinet who had unanimously subscribed to it. But Smuts apparently took the view that his commitment to a policy of neutrality did not extend beyond the immediate Munich crisis in September. A reassessment of the international situation in the light of recent developments would obviously release him from an earlier commitment. It would certainly demand a change of strategy. Neutrality did not guarantee immunity. Hertzog's declaration of neutrality was no more than a unilateral decision to keep out of war. Such a declaration – even when committed to writing – was no safeguard against the depredations of a ruthless aggressor. Smuts had at last come to the conclusion that Hitler was seeking to dominate the world by force and that there was no limit to his ambitions. A triumphant Hitler would annex South West Africa and reduce South Africa to a vassal state. The only safe course for South Africa, if she valued her freedom and independence, was to join in a concerted effort to overthrow Hitler. Moreover, Hertzog could not complain that Smuts had concealed his change of attitude. Smuts's recent speeches, prominently displayed and conspicuously headlined in the press, must have made it abundantly clear to his colleagues as well as to the public at large that he had repudiated a policy of neutrality and now insisted that South Africa should stand by her friends and associates in the Commonwealth in a war against Hitler.

On 1 September Hitler attacked Poland. The fateful moment had come. The following day the Cabinet met. Hertzog opened the proceedings and harangued the Cabinet steadily and relentlessly for more than an hour. The gist of it all was that 'Hitler was attempting nothing more than to free Germany from the fetters of Versailles and that South Africa should follow the policy of neutrality agreed upon at the time of the Munich crisis.' General Kemp, who spoke in support of Hertzog, declared that there would be a bloodbath in South Africa unless the Government maintained neutrality.

According to the account of Mr Harry Lawrence, who was present at the momentous meeting:

'General Smuts leant forward, his delicate hands ranging restlessly as was their wont in moments of emotion. He began by stating that the decision he had come to was the most serious he had been called upon to take in all his life; then he went on to say why South Africa should stand by the Commonwealth and declare war on Germany. Incidentally, he observed that he was Minister of Justice and he had no reason to think that a declaration of war would lead to a blood bath.' [37]

At the conclusion of the debate, a vote was taken and seven members of the Cabinet supported Smuts in favour of war, six supported Hertzog in favour of neutrality. The Cabinet was split down the middle. Hertzog adjourned the meeting to the following afternoon.

The adjourned meeting was very short. 'General Hertzog declared that he would put the matter to the House. He was obviously convinced that he would have a majority for his neutrality motion.' Smuts made it clear that he would come to the House with a counter-motion. There was nothing more to be said. The meeting ended, and after lingering on to exchange a few parting civilities over a glass of sherry, Hertzog and Smuts and their respective colleagues went their separate ways. The great moments in history are not always keyed to a high dramatic note.

The next scene took place in the House of Assembly. On Monday, 4 September, the members assembled to debate the momentous issue. It was impossible to predict the outcome of the debate. The fate of the country trembled in a most precarious balance.

Hertzog rose in a tense and silent House to move his resolution.

In essence the resolution was the same as the declaration of neutrality he had carefully drafted at the time of Munich, in September of the previous year; it proposed a neutrality modified to some extent to allow Britain and the Commonwealth to make use of the naval base at Simonstown and all the facilities of South Africa's ports and docks.

Speaking to his motion, Hertzog said:

'It is clear that this is a policy which not only aims at, but will result in the Union keeping out of war, but at the same time the Union will be fulfilling all its obligations with regard to the Commonwealth of Nations of which we are a member.' [38]

He then went on to explain that the Cabinet was divided on the issue, and the division was irreparable.

'If there were those', he said, probably turning a meaningful look towards Smuts, 'who differed from me, then I would have thought it was their duty, while there was time, while the people could still have been informed, to have spoken and to have stated their case. [He] did not deserve to be left in the lurch in such a critical time.'

He went on to argue that the issue was one of national independence; the outbreak of war was an opportunity for the Afrikaner people to uphold South Africa's sovereign independence – it was the crucial test.

'I have over and over again said to the people of South Africa that South Africa will not be plunged into any war unless the interests of South Africa are threatened . . . If it should happen that we should be dragged into war, it will be a catastrophe . . . there will be a state of misery in South Africa which will not be cured in fifty years . . . The Afrikaner nation has now made two attempts to bring together the Afrikaans-speaking section of the nation and the English-speaking section, to fuse them into one nation and I say that this failure of the second attempt to weld them into one people is enough to shock the people so deeply that it will take years for us to recover . . .'

He insisted that:

'. . . nobody can blame us, just as little as we can blame England for its declaration of war against Germany without first asking us whether we are prepared to participate. Just as little can you or any other nation complain if we feel in our hearts that what we do is in the interests of South Africa, and that we act in accordance with our convictions.'

Hertzog wanted a declaration of neutrality because it would establish South Africa's independence once and for all.

He spoke with passion and conviction and it appears that so far his speech made a deep impression on the House. South Africa could undoubtedly prove her independence by adopting a policy of neutrality. But would a policy of neutrality safeguard her independence? It was at this point that Hertzog began to overstate his case, no doubt in an effort to conceal its essential weakness. He reverted to the theme he had elaborated at the Cabinet meeting: he argued in effect that Germany was not the aggressor but the aggrieved and that Hitler's sole aim was to remove the evils of Versailles – the 'monster of Versailles' Hertzog called it – an aim with which he personally, as one who had also suffered the harsh consequences of defeat, could sympathise. Germany was therefore no menace to South Africa, and the war was not of the slightest concern to South Africa.

Smuts then rose to put his counter-motion. He began by saying that the difference between him and the Prime Minister concerned a matter which was of the gravest national importance.

'I have never in all these years of our political collaboration made a serious point of differences on small issues. I have always been prepared to give way, to hold the peace, and to see that the young life of the nation is given a chance and for the people to have an opportunity to grow together. Today we have come to a point where I have to call a halt and I have to adopt a different attitude, and I do so because I am in my soul convinced that we are against most vital issues for the present and for the future of this country.'

He made it clear that he too was moved solely by a concern for the interests of South Africa. Hertzog's argument that Hitler sought only to right the wrongs of Versailles and had no aims beyond the redress of Germany's grievances could not be sustained after the rape of Czechoslovakia. There were in fact no limits to Hitler's ambitions. Hitler's designs on Danzig and the corridor were

'part and parcel of this whole course on which the new Germany has set out to dominate the world by force and to annex as much as she can under threats of war . . . We have had due notice that the next demand after Danzig has been wiped off the slate is going to be the return of the German colonies . . . the question we have to face in this country is what is our position going to be within some months or some years when we are treated as Austria has been treated, as Czechoslovakia has been treated and as Poland is now being treated, when we are faced with superior force and we have to surrender what we consider to be vital in the interests of the Union, at the point of the bayonet.'

He concluded by saying that nothing would be more fatal to South Africa than to dissociate itself directly or indirectly from the rest of the Commonwealth on this crucial occasion.

'It is not only a question of loyalty and of the self-respect of South Africa which I assume we all feel deeply . . . we should do our duty, we should do the proper thing and align ourselves with our friends and we should ward off and prevent those dangers which are almost sure to overtake this country in the future if we now isolate ourselves and have afterwards to face our ordeal alone.'

Smuts, in arguing that if South Africa dissociated itself from the Commonwealth at this critical moment the time would come when she would find herself isolated in a dangerous world, presented a far more convincing case than Hertzog. But the effect of his speech was almost destroyed by the unfortunate contribution of Heaton Nicholls to the debate. According to Heaton Nicholls the issue was already decided; the Union was actually at war by virtue of the common allegiance which every British subject in the Commonwealth owed to the Crown.

'The country today is at war under our South African Constitution of which the King is part . . . Under the Act of Union the King of this country is the King of Great Britain and the Dominions, one and indivisible . . . In the Status Act we adopted a statement which was agreed to by the Prime Minister [which] said that these states of the British Commonwealth were linked together by a common allegiance to the Crown . . . You cannot owe anything in common and claim a right to act separately . . . Allegiance means something more than a mere word to be bandied about on political platforms, it has a very deep sacred significance, loyalty within the law to that common Crown. In the eyes of every English-speaking man in this country South Africa is at war; and it does not require any vote of this House or any declaration by the Government of this country to determine whether we are at war or not at war. The full right to determine the extent of our participation in that war is admitted. We cannot participate in any war, not a man can be moved except by a vote of this House, by money actually voted by Parliament. This is admitted throughout. The extent of our participation in a war is a matter entirely for Parliament to decide. But there is no doubt . . . we are at war in the eyes of every British subject, and if we are not at war, we cannot be British subjects . . . The Prime Minister, by his motion, is actually proposing secession from the Commonwealth, that and nothing more, secession from our common allegiance. If that should come about, secession will be fought in every possible manner by every loyal British subject in South Africa.'

Heaton Nicholls claimed that every constitutional authority throughout the British Commonwealth agreed with his interpretation of the Constitution; but nevertheless in basing his argument upon the constitutional position rather than on South Africa's vital interests, his speech made an unfortunate impression on the House. The mischief, however, was largely repaired by B. K. Long who, in a speech which was acclaimed as probably the most decisive contribution to the debate, upheld their right as representatives of a free and independent nation to decide the destiny of their country and, in effect, he repudiated Heaton Nicholls' claim that by virtue of their allegiance to the Crown they had not the right to do what the Prime Minister wanted to do. But, he went on to say that although he was convinced that they had the right to declare their neutrality he was equally profoundly convinced that it was disastrously unwise in the interests of their own country that they should take the course which the Prime Minister proposed.

'If we decide, whatever our decision may be in regard to the international situation, it will be our own decision, and if our decision is to join with Great Britain in this war . . . it would be our own decision, and we shall not be dragged in at the heels of Great Britain.'

Long then explained in cogent detail how South Africa's freedom and independence – cherished by English and Afrikaners alike, for they were both descended from a liberty-loving race – would be endangered by a victorious Germany.

'We are gambling here when we are talking about neutrality, we are gambling on the success of the British Commonwealth in this war while we are at the same time trying to refuse to take any part . . . that may be a possible course, but can it be said to be an honourable course? Is it not really an attempt to make the best of both worlds with the result that we shall get the worst of both worlds . . . There is not only a material price for this neutrality, there is also a moral price. In effect, if we carry this resolution of the Prime Minister we are going back on our friends, we are refusing to place ourselves on their side, we are saying to them "Well, you take on the burden of this war and fight for us and when you win then give us everything you have been accustomed to give in the past". There is a moral price we shall pay whether the British Commonwealth wins in this war or whether Germany wins. If the British Commonwealth wins the moral price that we shall pay is to be stigmatised before every free nation in the world as having failed to carry out our duty as a freedom-loving country and to join with our friends in the defence of freedom and liberty. If Germany wins do you think she is going to respect this neutrality of ours . . . That is a very, very dangerous assumption. Let Hon. Members read the letter which Herr Hitler wrote only three days ago to M. Daladier, the Prime Minister of France. Let them see how he talked about Danzig and his grievances against the Poles; let them substitute for Danzig in each case and each sentence the words South West Africa and then they will know what the fate of this country will be in case Germany, which God forbid, should win this war. We can expect no mercy, we shall be an object of contempt to that ruthless nation which only respects those who stand up for their own rights.

We shall be regarded as having failed to stand up for our friends and any fate which befalls us is but our own desert. I shudder when I think what the consequences to our country will be if in this war the forces of the British Commonwealth are defeated.'

Malan followed Long. He endorsed Hertzog's justification of Hitler and argued that Germany's annexation of Czechoslovakia was 'a matter of safety' – an extraordinary justification for an act of aggression, for it meant that Germany was morally entitled to inflict on Czechoslovakia the wrongs which Versailles, as 'a matter of safety', had inflicted on Germany!

The division bell rang at nine o'clock that evening. When the count was taken, Smuts gained a majority of thirteen over Hertzog. The Dominion Party, the Labour Party and the three Native Representatives together with the pro-war wing of the United Party gave Smuts his victory. The majority of the United Party had in fact voted for Hertzog's resolution.

Hertzog requested the Governor-General, Sir Patrick Duncan, to dissolve Parliament and hold a general election. The Governor-General, however, took the view that the voting in Parliament had shown that Smuts had sufficient support to form a government and therefore there was no need to consult the electorate.

Smuts promptly formed a coalition government; in acknowledgment of the support he had received from the Dominion Party and the Labour Party he brought Stallard and Madeley into the Cabinet. He also brought back Hofmeyr and Sturrock, the former as Minister of Finance and the latter as Minister of Transport. Smuts, once more in control of affairs, now had to face the destiny of a country at war.

XIV

Thus fusion came to its inevitable end. To bring about fusion Smuts had sacrificed the premiership which was within his reach and had accepted a subordinate role under General Hertzog. But was fusion a success? Did it confer a lasting benefit on the country? Could Smuts look back upon it with any degree of satisfaction, with a sense of personal achievement? Fusion has acquired a legendary glamour. The years of fusion are still referred to, nostalgically, as a 'golden age'. To question whether fusion was worthwhile is regarded as rank heresy: to doubt the purity of Smuts's motives in seeking to promote it and making it his 'lifework' is regarded as the mark of a cynical mind.

It is true that under the fusion Government the country enjoyed a period of unprecedented prosperity. But the prosperity was entirely due to the rise in the price of gold, which Hertzog had delayed, almost disastrously, by clinging to the gold standard. The prosperity of the gold-mines and its abundant overspill into the other sectors of the economy would have redounded to the credit of any Government fortunate enough to be in power at the time. If Smuts had stood out against 'reunion' and had formed his own Government – a purely South African Party Government – the glory would have been entirely his – and with far more justification.

Unfortunately, circumstances, becoming coercive in character, had made him decide in favour of reunion. His sacrifice, although an unwilling sacrifice, would have been worthwhile if his reconciliation with Hertzog had ushered in a new and creative epoch, and, if under a fusion government, Briton and Boer had learned to live and work together in the spirit of a united nation.

But fusion was not destined to endure. From the first it had within it the seeds of disruption. It had no inner cohesion; it was not held together by a fundamental principle acting as a unifying force. It was not an organic union, born of a genuine community of interests and ideals. It was a mechanical coming together of two parties, an arrangement – a marriage of convenience – dictated by political expediency and glorified by wishful thinking into a semblance of something less spurious than, in essence, it really was. For a time Hertzog and Smuts succeeded, by a conspiracy of silence on basic issues, in giving it a semblance of unity. When, however, with the advent of war, these basic issues flared into life, its surface integument was not strong enough to hold it together. Fusion burst asunder. And the bitter aftermath produced divisions far more fundamental and irreconcilable than the differences which had kept Smuts and Hertzog at enmity for twenty years.

In short, fusion did not fulfil the high historic purpose for which it was acclaimed. It was an episode, a brief and, on the surface, a bright interlude in the political history of South Africa. It was founded on the assumption that a reconciliation between Smuts and Hertzog would be strong enough to guarantee its stability. And indeed, Smuts, in order to maintain an unbroken surface of unity, had to identify himself with reactionary measures and lend himself to political manoeuvres which caused him humiliation, did almost irreparable damage to his reputation and diminished his stature in the eyes of his most ardent admirers. With the advent of war, the fundamental issues – neutrality, the divisibility of the crown, the right to secede – became issues of burning importance. Hidden and irreconcilable differences – causes of tension within the United Party – were forced into the open. Smuts was compelled at last to take a decisive stand. It was a fateful stand. It committed South Africa to the crusade against Hitlerism. But its immediate effect was to shatter the hollow fabric of fusion, to the dismay of those who had persuaded themselves that national unity had been established on firm and lasting foundations. For Smuts, it was an act of deliverance. It freed him from his thraldom to Hertzog and, in one dramatic stroke, restored him to the summit of power.

NOTES

[1] People's Leader.

[2] The Balfour Declaration read as follows: 'Great Britain and the self-governing dominions are autonomous communities within the British Empire, equal in status, in no way subordinate one to another in any aspect of their internal or external affairs, though united by common allegiance to the Crown and freely associated as members of the British Commonwealth of Nations.'

[3] The price of gold rose from £4 4s. to £6 and later to £7 an ounce.

[4] Reunion.

[5] Big Barn, the official residence of the Prime Minister, originally the home of Cecil Rhodes.

[6] True.

[7] One land, one people, one language.

Section Three

Decline and Fall

. . . To reaffirm faith in fundamental human rights, in the dignity and worth of the human person, in the equal rights of men and women of nations large and small . . .

J. C. Smuts, Preamble to
Charter of the United Nations

I

The general election of 1943 resulted in a victory for General Smuts. It was the greatest triumph of his career. The election was fought on the war issue and it was fought at the right moment. The successful conclusion of the campaign in North Africa – to which the South African forces made a magnificent contribution – the impending invasion of Italy and the retreat of the German armies in Russia were portents of a final victory. These favourable events on the battle-fronts ensured an overwhelming electoral triumph for Smuts over an opposition which had consistently opposed his war-effort and predicted defeat for the Allied cause. In the new Parliament his following increased to 110 in a house of 160. The Opposition was reduced to 43. As a result of an electoral pact with Smuts the Labour Party increased its representation from 4 to 9. The Dominion Party retained its 7 seats, all but one of which were in Natal. The country had fully endorsed Smuts's war policy, and South Africa's participation in the war was decisively vindicated.

Thus, after the general election of 1943, Smuts was at the height of his power. The position of the United Party was unassailable. Throughout the war years Smuts stood firmly by the Allied cause; confident of final victory, he not only organised a superb war-effort as South Africa's contribution to the winning of the war, but rendered valuable service to Churchill at the vital centre of operations. In recognition of his immense personal contribution to the war-effort he was honoured by the King who conferred upon him the rank of Field Marshal. His reputation overseas was now higher than ever. His oracular utterances were received with universal acclaim. At the London Guildhall in October 1943 he delivered probably the finest speech of his career; confident of the success of the final offensive against Germany, he ended on a high prophetic note – 'Let the greatest war in human history become the prelude to the greatest peace. To make it such will be the greatest glory of our age and its noblest bequest to the generations to come.'

The collapse of Germany's armed resistance in 1945 and the consequent end of hostilities in Europe created the opportunity for building the new world-order of which he spoke with such prophetic fervour. Smuts was ready to make his contribution. He led the Union delegation at the inauguration of the United Nations Organisation at San Francisco. He was entrusted with the task of drafting the Preamble to the United Nations Charter, a historic task for which, it was generally agreed, he was uniquely qualified and which he accomplished with great distinction. South Africa was proud of him, and on his return home he received a great popular welcome, acclaimed by his followers and admirers with wild enthusiasm. Only the Opposition held aloof – they treated his efforts to build a new world-organisation with scorn, predicting that the United Nations would end as the League of Nations had ended, in futility and failure.

Smuts could afford to ignore his opponents. His star was definitely in the ascendant. After the general election of 1943 he was at the height of his power. After V.E. day – victory in

Europe – he was at the height of his prestige. He had brought his country through years of bitter adversity to ultimate triumph. At home, his authority as Prime Minister was complete and unchallengeable; he was in full control of the destiny of his country. Abroad his prestige was immense – no other Commonwealth statesman, outside of Britain, had ever attained such heights.

Alas! from those heights there was a sharp decline. Three short years later, he fell from power. He was rejected by the electorate and had to yield office to his political opponents who had opposed his participation in the war, derided the men in the armed forces, rejoiced in the Allies' reverses, had demanded a separate peace with Hitler and declared openly that the future of South Africa depended on a Nazi victory. Smuts's fall was not only a personal tragedy, but because of its consequences for South Africa, it constituted a national disaster.

II

What went wrong? How did it happen? Why was he dethroned from his unique position? Why with all the power at his command, did he fail to establish a new direction which would have made it impossible for the reactionary forces, who had bitterly opposed his war-effort, to rise to power and defeat the aims for which the war was fought? Why did he not exercise the strong leadership of which he was undoubtedly capable, to prevent such a disaster? Why was it possible for these reactionary forces, whom he had vanquished in 1943, to return in triumph and reduce all his achievements to dust?

During the last phase of the war and its immediate aftermath, his preoccupations overseas left him little or no time to attend to the demands of the domestic situation. It was to his credit and in keeping with his stature that he should recognise and accept responsibilities beyond the shores of South Africa – heavy and exacting responsibilities. But the problems which faced him at home were no less challenging and claimed the highest place in his scheme of priorities. He had dedicated himself to the task of building a new world-order; but was it logical to assume that he could play a leading part in the reconstruction of the world and leave the structure of society in South Africa unchanged and unaffected? He must have realised that his work in the international sphere entailed upon him a parallel obligation on the home front. But strangely enough, whilst he devoted himself with enthusiasm to the work of building a new world-order, his prophetic fervour seemed to desert him when he was confronted with his domestic tasks. In the sphere of home affairs, he had no clear vision of the future. He made no attempt to project a programme, promising measures more durable than stop-gap devices and goals more practical than Utopian dreams, which would inspire confidence in the United Party as an instrument of social change.

There was also a striking contrast between the sustained and concentrated effort he had devoted to the business of waging war and his irresolute, almost haphazard, approach to the problems of peace. Where the war-effort was concerned, he acted decisively and purposefully; he sought out the best brains for each specific task; he delegated the necessary authority to the men he selected and supported their efforts to the hilt. As a result, starting from scratch, he recruited, organised, trained and equipped a first-class fighting force which made a splendid contribution to the winning of the war. Unfortunately he made no comparable effort to 'win the peace'. Smuts was content to face the aftermath of war and its manifold problems without making any changes in his cabinet. He was prepared to carry on with the same unimpressive team, described as 'the weakest Government the Union has ever had'. The very fact that his overseas commitments made it impossible for Smuts to give his undivided attention to home affairs, made it all the more imperative to ensure that their management was placed in capable hands. Hofmeyr, about the only one in the Cabinet on whom Smuts could rely, was indeed an outstanding administrator. But Hofmeyr was already overburdened with work; and, in any case, Smuts would allow Hofmeyr to exercise no authority beyond the administrative field. In matters of policy, Smuts was the sole arbiter. Hofmeyr, acting under no dynamic policy directive, could do no more than ensure that during Smuts's frequent and sometimes prolonged absence the machinery of Government ran smoothly and efficiently.

After the election of 1943, there was no lack of able young back-benchers whom Smuts could have brought into the Government. They would have given his Cabinet a 'new look', a new dynamism, at a time when an imaginative and bold reconstruction of his Cabinet would have been highly appropriate and a sign that a regenerative force was at work in the United Party.

When Smuts led South Africa into the war against Hitler he regained in full measure the prestige which, during the period of his eclipse by Hertzog, had sadly waned. The young men who entered Parliament in 1943 had fought the election under his banner with renewed faith in his leadership. They had offered themselves as candidates for Parliament in a spirit of idealism; they pledged themselves to support Smuts not only in the struggle against the totalitarian powers, but in his work for peace; they dedicated themselves to the task of building a new society which, conceived in the spirit of the Atlantic Charter, would give meaning and purpose to all the sorrow and sacrifice involved in the war, a new society which would enable all sections of the community to make their full contribution to its progress and prosperity and share more generously in the expanded resources of the country.

Theirs was a noble and inspiring dream. Like young crusaders, their lances at the ready, they waited for an opportunity to go into action. The opportunity never came. Smuts showed no sign that he was even aware of their existence. He made no attempt to create openings for them either by enlarging the Cabinet – an appropriate step in view of the manifold problems that were emerging in the post-war epoch – or, better still, by retiring some of the old hacks who constituted the majority of the Cabinet; nor did he think of creating junior ministerial posts which would have enabled young men to gain valuable experience before elevating them to the Cabinet. It was with his existing team of mediocrities that Smuts was prepared to carry on and face the challenge of the future. With the exception of Hofmeyr, they all stood in awe of Smuts, and their chief merit was that they were ready to render him an unquestioning obedience. Smuts, firmly established in the driver's seat, wanted a team obedient to the rein; young blood might set too hot a pace and – who knows? – might even take the bit between their teeth. One Hofmeyr in the team was enough.

So these young men – the new men with the new ideas – sat on the back-benches and watched their elders and betters go into action. The spectacle was not edifying. There was Conroy, the Minister of Lands, pugnacious and easily thrown off balance in debate, allowing himself to be provoked by the Malanites into a tactless tirade against their Church. There was poor old Clarkson, the slow-witted Minister of the Interior, trying to extricate himself from an unhappy situation by agreeing with his critics on every side of the House until he stood helplessly enmeshed in a self-spun web of contradictions. There was Piet van der Bijl, the Minister of Native Affairs, floundering in deep waters as he tried to articulate a meaningful reply to the Native Representatives who stated their case in terms of a political philosophy much above his comprehension. With few opportunities of entering into the debates themselves, the young back-benchers sat there, embarrassed by the ineptitude of the men whom Smuts had entrusted with great responsibilities. Their enthusiasm gradually evaporated, to be replaced by a sense of frustration. And so the young men who had embellished their election manifestos with emotive phrases about the brave new world they intended to build, saw no bright prospect of change under Smuts.

These young men, however, derived some encouragement from the presence of Hofmeyr in the Cabinet; they felt that under his leadership the liberal element would gather strength and exert influence on the United Party from within. But Hofmeyr's position in the Party was somewhat anomalous. A professed liberal, Hofmeyr's lack of passionate commitment during this period gave his admirers as much ground for disappointment as for hope. As a member of the fusion Government he had not hesitated, on several important occasions, to take a stand on grounds of principle, and although it brought him into conflict with Smuts it was essentially against the policies of Hertzog that he had rebelled. When he received a call from Smuts to serve in the war Cabinet, he responded with alacrity; he was grateful for the opportunity to make his contribution to the war-effort and felt that he owed a special loyalty to Smuts for giving a decisive lead to the Nation on the war issue. He therefore devoted himself with unremitting diligence to his administrative tasks and was extremely reluctant, in matters of policy, to deviate from the line laid down by Smuts. Hofmeyr was conscious of the fact that he had an eager following in the Party, but felt that they must be kept in check; and so he was careful to avoid differences, on questions of policy, which might sow the seeds of a revolt against Smuts. He was not prepared at this stage to encourage the growth of a dissident group in the caucus, for such a development might culminate in a premature split in the United Party. His followers however were not discouraged; they hung on session after session in the hope that Hofmeyr might succeed Smuts or, more likely, in the hope that Hofmeyr, faced at last with an issue on which he would have to take a decisive stand, would break away from the United Party and unfurl his own banner as the rallying point for a great liberal revival.

And what of the official Opposition? There is no doubt that the weakness of the Government did much to restore the fighting spirit of the Nationalists at a time when their political fortunes were at a low ebb. After 1943 the certain prospect of a German defeat had a palpable influence on the Opposition. By V.E. day they were visibly crestfallen. It was apparent that the defeat of Hitler, on whose ultimate triumph they had staked their political fortunes, had dealt them a devastating blow. The United Party however failed to exploit this advantage to the full. Conscious of their inadequacies, they were too ready to derive comfort from the assumption that history had decided the fate of the Opposition and that verbal triumphs in debate could scarcely add to the discomfiture of the Nationalists. They greatly underestimated the resourcefulness and resiliency of the Opposition.

The Nationalists quickly and skilfully trimmed their sails to the post-war wind. They were at great pains to disavow any sympathy for Nazism. They declared that they had been neutral and not pro-German in their attitude to the war. With a cynical disregard for their former attitude, they showed a disposition to take a friendly interest in the welfare of the returned soldier. They even quoted the English poets in praise of democracy. They knew how to exploit the weakness of the Government in debate; they drew both strength and encouragement from the ineptitude of the Ministers they faced. At first, rather tentatively, and then, as their reactionary views went unchallenged, more blatantly, they returned to the attack. They imposed their strategy upon the Government. They chose their favourite battleground – the field of race relations, where their appeal to colour prejudice would dominate the debates. By the time they reached the second session – the notorious session of 1945, devoted almost entirely to questions of colour – it was clear that in the struggle for the ascendancy over the minds of the electorate the initiative was passing to the Opposition. And it soon got around that 'man for man the Nationalist front-benchers were superior to Smuts's team'. Clearly, the Nationalists were gaining acceptance as an alternative Government!

It was soon apparent that Smuts, thrown on the defensive by an aggressive Opposition, was more concerned about maintaining the status quo than attempting a bold forward movement in the field of policy and planning. In Parliament the progressive point of view found no adequate expression. The liberals in the United Party, who represented the forces of change, had no influence either on policy or legislation. In the absence of a decisive lead from Smuts, the old guard of the United Party adopted a purely defensive posture – although, since South Africa's participation in the war was by this time fully vindicated, precisely what they were defending was not at all clear, save perhaps a few tattered remants of policy inherited from the halcyon days of fusion, such as Anglo-Afrikaner co-operation and the 'final settlement of 1936'. The fight in Parliament between the Government and the Opposition resolved itself into a contest between the defenders of an ill-defined status quo and the protagonists of a traditional way of life which derived its values and inspiration from the historic past – from the struggles of the Voortrekkers to preserve the ascendancy of an exclusive and isolationist Afrikaner Nationalism.

Whilst this almost archaic fight was going on between the Government and the Opposition, Parliament was completely out of touch with the trend of events in the world outside. In Parliament, the liberal element, who represented the forces of change, were reduced to impotence; outside Parliament change was actually in progress. It was this dichotomy – a dichotomy between politics and economics – that rendered Parliament unresponsive to the demands of a dynamic and changing society.

For South Africa was experiencing the repetition of a historic process. It was undergoing an industrial revolution; it was advancing from feudalism to capitalism. A change in the method of production was transforming the Natives from a primitive peasantry into an urban proletariat. The integration of the Natives into the economic life of the country was an inevitable response to the demands of industrial development, and it was clear that this process of integration would accelerate as the economy expanded.

Liberal theoreticians, on the alert for signs of change, were quick to recognise that this process of economic integration was a factor of fundamental and far-reaching importance. It encouraged the most sanguine hopes. Liberalism as a political doctrine, relying chiefly on its ethical appeal and operating independently of economic forces, had fought a losing battle. Where liberal ideas had failed to penetrate, economic forces, always irresistible, would open the door to progress. The complete interdependence of White and Black in a modern expanding economy would ensure the emergence of a common society. Economic integration made nonsense of the segregation policy on which the 1936 legislation was based. Hertzog's dream of a 'final settlement' was finally shattered. The key to progress was to recognise economic integration as an irreversible process, to accept its political implications and plan accordingly.

No one understood all this more clearly than Smuts. In February 1942 he delivered a significant address to the Institute of Race Relations. His main theme was the social consequences of large-scale industrialisation and urbanisation.

Smuts acknowledged at the outset that in South Africa the Whites, being a small minority, were subject to 'the motive of fear' which was a complicating factor in the field of race relations.

'Attempts, as you know, have been made to get round this fear by the policy commonly called segregation – the policy of keeping Europeans and Africans completely apart for their own self-preservation. We have tried to carry out this policy. Legislation giving effect to it has been placed on the Statute Book. But I am afraid that there is very great disappointment at the result which has been achieved. Our fervent hope that fears would be allayed and that everybody would find his place – that Whites and Blacks would live happily in this country – has not been realised yet. The high expectations that we entertained of that policy have been sadly disappointed.

'How can it be otherwise? The whole trend both in this country and throughout Africa has been in the opposite direction. The whole movement of development here on this continent has been for closer contacts to be established between the various races and the various sections of the community.

'Isolation has gone and segregation has fallen on evil days . . .

'But there are other phenomena springing out of these conditions. You have what I may call the urbanisation of the Natives. A revolutionary change is taking place among the Native peoples of Africa through the movement from the country to the towns . . . the movement from the old Reserves in the Native areas to the big European centres of population. Segregation tried to stop it. It has, however, not stopped it in the least. The process has been accelerated. You might as well try to sweep the ocean back with a broom . . .' [1]

Smuts's speech caused a great stir. It was regarded as a speech of epoch-making importance. Surely, if logic was a compulsive element in his thinking, he would in due course announce a fundamental change of policy. It was certainly expected of him after the election victory of 1943. His position was unassailable. He was in full command of the political situation. Would he exercise strong leadership and establish a new direction in the field of race relations? Would he 'make straight the way' to a common society?

These expectations, however, were too buoyant. The real question, of course, was how would Smuts face up to the Nationalist Opposition on this issue? Malan too regarded Smuts's address as highly significant. He and his followers launched a fierce attack on Smuts for his apparent rejection of segregation. Was he prepared to allow the indiscriminate mingling of the races in the big cities – in the urban areas? In the session of 1945 Malan, making colour politics the main subject of debate, made it clear even at that stage that colour would be the dominant theme in the next election, due in 1948. He demanded to know where Smuts stood in the matter of segregation. Quoting extensively from Smuts's speech to the Institute of Race Relations, he said:

'Seeing the Prime Minister holds that view about the segregation policy – which was South Africa's traditional policy – seeing that he holds that view – I am entitled to ask . . . Tell us and tell the country where South Africa is going. I want to stress the following . . . If you take away the segregation policy you are not only going to give the Natives an equal status with the White man, but you are going to create a radical change in the relationship towards the Native and so far as his relationship towards the European is concerned. Whither South Africa?' [2]

Smuts, in his reply, began with an earnest plea to keep the colour question out of the political arena:

'The colour question . . . is the most serious social problem in South Africa. It affects the whole structure of our community, and it is a matter which we must discuss from the broad point of view and not merely from the point of view of party politics . . . Elections have been contested on the Black danger. No progress has been made along those lines. As long as the question of colour is a football in party politics, no progress will be made, and what I am about to say will be entirely outside the sphere of party politics.'

He then went on to deal with the Hertzog legislation of 1936:

'That legislation was passed nine years ago and many people thought . . . that the Native question in South Africa would be solved along those lines . . . But the Native problem is not a static question . . . and although we thought nine years ago that we had done a good thing and that we had chosen a firm policy for the future which would probably solve the Native question, we were very soon disillusioned . . . The position in the country has changed tremendously and that position has had its reaction on the Native question . . . Industrialisation in this country during the past ten or twenty years has gone ahead at an astounding rate. We no longer have the old position in South Africa where the Natives lived in their Reserves, and then went out to work in the mines, to work in the cities and also on the farms . . . Large numbers of natives are drawn to the cities. That is a natural development. It will continue to take place on an increasing scale . . . We shall need all our powers in South Africa to accomplish the task which is ahead of us in connection with an industrial expansion.'

Smuts then dwelt at length and rather discursively on the many problems created by the great influx of Natives into the urban areas. And he concluded by saying:

'I am in favour of dealing with this question with which we are faced on a basis which will not shock public opinion in this country or overseas, which will not give rise to a feeling of injustice in the mind of the Coloured person or the Native . . . There is no reason for concern about the future as long as we do our duty and do justice to all sections of the community and do our best to solve practical questions in a practical and reasonable manner.' [3]

As a major policy-statement, Smuts's speech was cautious, non-committal and unconstructive; it was positive only in his final assurance that White supremacy would be maintained and the social separation of the races in the urban areas would be enforced.

It was clear that in Parliament, face to face with the Opposition, Smuts was not prepared to take the bold course which his famous address to the Institute of Race Relations seemed to presage. His reply to Malan, if not a retreat from the position he had taken up on that memorable occasion, certainly gave no indication of a decisive and purposeful advance.

The explanation is that Smuts was never, at any time, ready to move in advance of public opinion. That was the chief of his shortcomings as a statesman. A political leader who is determined to use his party as an instrument of social change must recognise that one of his main functions is to create a favourable climate for change. In other words, he must lead and influence public opinion. And the measure of his success in this endeavour will be the measure of his achievement as a statesman. If he is content to head a party which merely reflects current ideas and prejudices, he is following public opinion, not leading it. It is true of course that a political leader who runs too far ahead of public opinion will reduce his following and end up in sectarian impotence. Just how far ahead of public opinion he can afford to go at any time is a delicate and difficult question to decide and is the test of his political acumen. Smuts, however, tended to err on the side of caution. In his address to the Institute, he had brought himself to the point where he was prepared to accept economic integration as an irreversible process, but he was not prepared to accept its logical implications and plan accordingly. He had, in his address, urged that in the sphere of health, housing and education much more must be done for the Natives; but he was not prepared to recognise that, as a permanent part of the urban population, the Natives had a claim to rights over and above the claims dictated by elementary human needs. He was not prepared to acknowledge that they had a claim to citizenship status, to a share in the making of the laws which governed them, to a right, as workers, to bargain for their living standards through recognised trade unions. And to a right to own and occupy a house in the area where they were permanently settled.

In a word, although Smuts clearly understood the nature of the challenge that confronted him, he was not prepared to formulate a broad and bold policy to meet it. Instead he adopted the time-honoured expedient of the cautious statesman. He appointed a Commission of Inquiry. Under the chairmanship of Mr Justice Fagan, a former Minister of Native Affairs, the Commission was given wide terms of reference. Broadly speaking, it was to inquire into the existing laws relating to the Natives in or near the urban areas, the operation of the pass laws, the employment in mines and other industries of migrant labour and its social and economic effects, and to draft such legislation as might be necessary to give effect to its recommendations.

Smuts was aware that the report of the Commission would tell him what he already knew and would confirm what he had elaborated in his address to the Institute of Race Relations. Politically, however, the Commission would serve a useful purpose. It would remove the Native question from the area of debate. As far as the liberals were concerned, it would nourish the hope that its recommendations would favour the changes they sought. It would fend off the Opposition attack; they would have to hold their fire until the Government announced its attitude to the Commission's recommendations. And finally the report would prepare the public mind for any changes in Native policy which Smuts might initiate and it would thus create a favourable climate for the reception of any legislation it would entail.

In short, by appointing a Commission, Smuts hoped to gain time. But unfortunately for Smuts time was not on his side, especially as he had to contend with an Opposition who, despite his earnest plea, were not prepared to oblige him by keeping the Native question out of the sphere of party politics. They were not prepared to surrender their most powerful political weapon. In fact they took full advantage of his inaction; they proclaimed that Smuts had no policy, and that he was intent only on jettisoning the traditional policy of segregation which, ever since the days of the Voortrekkers, had kept South Africa safe for the White man. Moreover, events do not wait on the findings of a commission. He had disposed of the Native question for the time being by submitting it to the scrutiny of the Fagan Commission. But the affairs of the

Indian community became a matter of serious concern, calling for immediate action.

III

As Smuts had no comprehensive plan for dealing with the many problems in the all-important field of race relations, he was compelled to meet each of these problems as it arose and in accordance with its degree of urgency. He had now to cope with the problem of Indian penetration into the European areas, which had become a burning issue in Natal, particularly in Durban. The dimensions of the trouble, which actually began in 1943, were indicated in his own words:

'At the moment we are busy with a Bill to stabilise the Indian situation in Durban where there is wild excitement because rich Indians have been buying up properties on a large scale in the heart of Durban and panic has set in among the Europeans. You know the sort of situation and the fear which naturally possesses the Whites on such occasions. There is nothing for it but to peg the position and forbid property transfer there for three years so that the whole position can be judicially enquired into. But this again has created commotion among Indians here and in India and moved the Indian Government to do its bit in the general hue and cry . . . I can never get away from this Indian tangle and the troubles of East and West.' [4]

Smuts's decision to stabilise the Indian situation resulted in the enactment of the Trading and Occupation of Land (Transvaal and Natal) Restrictions Bill, known as the Pegging Act. It was described as an interim measure, but it renewed the restrictions which had been imposed four years earlier upon Indians in the Transvaal and which were also intended to be of a temporary nature. The Pegging Act deprived Indians of legal rights which had been granted to them as far back as 1865 and which they had enjoyed ever since then. Needless to say, the Act not only provoked the bitter resentment of the local Indian community, but was denounced in the most irate terms in India.

Smuts appointed a Commission of Inquiry under Mr Justice Broome, with a balanced membership of two Indians and three Europeans and with wide powers to examine every aspect of the Indian situation in Durban. Arising out of the work of the Commission, Mr A. I. Kajee, one of its Indian members and a highly respected member of the Indian community, noted for his moderation, drew up a plan which he offered as a compromise. The essence of his plan was that in the urban areas the Indians would enjoy unrestricted rights of land purchase and ownership but they would voluntarily accept restrictions upon their rights of residence; a mixed Board consisting of two Europeans and two Indians with a European Chairman would control and issue licences of occupation. The merit of his plan lay in the fact that the Indians were prepared to make a substantial concession which would involve no surrender of principle; and it would establish a method of co-operation between Europeans and Indians in matters of common concern. The plan immediately commended itself to Smuts as a highly satisfactory solution and he formally accepted it in Pretoria on 18 April 1944.

Smuts was highly pleased with the Pretoria agreement. 'He sent telegrams to the Viceroy and the Secretary of State – his friends Wavell and Amery – summarising the agreement and expressing the conviction that it would be as welcome to them as it was to him.' [5]

Smuts then left for the Commonwealth Conference in London and for the conference in San Francisco to make his contribution to the work of establishing the United Nations. But immediately upon his leaving the country Natal rose in revolt against the Pretoria agreement.

The revolt was in fact instigated by the Dominion Party. By joining the coalition Government under Smuts, the Dominion Party, whose special concern was the Crown and the Commonwealth, had in a sense lost its distinctive role. All parties in the coalition had vindicated their loyalty to the Crown and proved their attachment to the Commonwealth. Concerned about its viability as a party when the coalition terminated, the Dominion Party sought an issue on which it could speak with an authentic voice of its own. It was chiefly a Natal Party and the Indian problem was largely a Natal problem. Here then was an opportunity to exploit a highly incendiary issue. It led the agitation against Indian encroachment on the White man's preserves, and soon nearly all the Whites of Natal were involved in the hue and cry. Thus the Dominion Party, so zealous in its concern for the Commonwealth, instigated an agitation which was not only damaging to race relations in the country but to Commonwealth relations as well. Matters rose to a climax when the Ratepayers Association of Durban appealed to the Nationalists of the Orange Free State to come to their assistance and support them in their efforts to resist the Asiatic invasion. It was a shameful agitation; and it was a bitter irony that immediately after a war against Nazism the Whites of Natal should believe that a quarter of a million Indians could destroy Western civilisation in South Africa or give it an Asiatic orientation. Such a conception was in fact on a par with the notion that the small Jewish community in Germany constituted a menace to her Nordic culture.

Inevitably the Indians started a counter-agitation. The politically conscious younger generation of Indians, now thoroughly militant, repudiated the moderate leaders who sat on the Broome Commission and denounced the spirit of compromise which had led to the Pretoria Agreement. They succeeded in gaining control of the Natal Indian Congress and from that authoritative platform they proclaimed their demands in a ten-point programme inspired by the terms of the Atlantic Charter. Their programme, in effect, resolved itself into a demand for immediate equality.

The Broome Commission suffered the resignation of its Indian members and was now virtually defunct. The Chairman, however, issued an interim report which offered two suggestions for making a fresh start – firstly a conference between the Indian and South African Governments, and, secondly, a qualified franchise for the Indians on the common roll. Smuts rejected the first suggestion; it would, in his view, serve no useful purpose. He, however, adopted the second suggestion in a modified form; he would concede the franchise to Indians but not on the common roll; he would give them representation on a separate or communal roll.

In the Session of 1946 Smuts introduced the Asiatic Land Tenure and Indian Representation Bill. This measure perpetuated the restrictions imposed upon the purchase and tenure of land by Indians, but as a *quid pro quo* it gave them representation in Parliament and the Natal Provincial Council on a separate roll. It gave them the right to elect three representatives to Parliament provided they were White. It was a thoroughly reactionary measure, redeemed to some extent by the franchise proposals. Smuts hoped to keep himself in countenance as a liberal statesman by insisting that if the property restrictions were passed, the franchise proposals must be passed also.

Smuts, in introducing the Bill, spoke in terms which suggested that it was part of a grand design which represented his vision of the future. 'What we want', he said, 'is to establish an order of things under which the various communities in our society can live peacefully and quietly together.' It was a laudable aim, but it is the very essence of the indictment against Smuts that he had no such design for a new order. The Bill was dictated by expediency; it was not the product of some majestic conception in the sphere of race relations.

After his opening flourish, Smuts went on to say 'That is what we intend in this Bill – fair play and justice for our Indian fellow-citizens, but we do not want to change the structure of our society . . . we want to preserve the European orientation of our society.' [6]

The Nationalist Opposition, firmly attached to the principle of compulsory segregation as the only sound policy-pattern for a multi-racial society, were less concerned with 'fair-play and justice' for the Indian than with the preservation of the 'European orientation of our society' – a phrase which they accepted as a political euphemism for White supremacy. In their view, the restrictions on the purchase and tenure of property were not severe enough and the franchise proposals were too liberal. They argued that the granting of the communal franchise to the Indians would lead inevitably to further political demands from the other sections of the non-

European population; it was therefore a complete capitulation to a misguided liberalism (personified by Hofmeyr) and thus a threat to White civilisation.

Needless to say, the Dominion Party kept up a relentless attack on the Bill and vied with the Nationalists in seeking to make the land restrictions even more severe. They were convinced that they were engaged in an epic struggle to save White Natal from being overwhelmed by the Asiatic hordes who were threatening its very existence.

Hofmeyr, speaking for the liberals in the United Party, accepted the Bill as a compromise. 'It is because this Bill concedes political rights that I am prepared to accept it,' said Hofmeyr. 'Hitherto our history on the political side in our dealings with the Indian people in South Africa has been one of whittling away of rights. This Bill reverses the process of a whittling away of rights; we start giving back the rights we have taken away.' He went on to say that whilst he was not happy with the communal franchise 'he realised that it was not practicable to go further than we are going at present. It is the communal franchise or nothing.' Finally, he confidently predicted that, as far as representation in Parliament was concerned, the colour bar would eventually go and Indians would be represented by Indians. [7]

Hofmeyr made it clear that he accepted the Bill not as a final solution but as a compromise. But whatever value the communal franchise may have had as a compromise or as a *quid pro quo*, it had no intrinsic merit. A communal franchise would compel the Indian to vote not as an individual citizen in accordance with his material or economic interests, but as the member of a racial group. For a communal franchise assumes that all Indians whether rich or poor, merchants or labourers, employers or employees have an identity of interests simply because they have the same racial origin. Where a group, as in the case of the Natives, is still fairly simple and homogeneous in its social structure, a communal franchise can still be made to serve a purpose; its elected representatives can at least speak for the group as a whole. But this form of franchise is obviously unsuited to the complex social and economic structure of the Indian community which, in point of fact, is as stratified and diversified as the White community. A communal franchise would also tend to perpetuate the existing political alignments which are determined by race and not, as in every healthy and progressive society, by economic forces. However, despite its grave deficiencies, a communal franchise might have proved acceptable to the Indians if they had been given the right to send their own Indian spokesmen to Parliament. The fact that the Bill compelled them to elect White M.P.s as their representatives heightened the affront to the Indian community.

In the face of strong opposition and despite the fact that many of his own party disliked the Bill, Smuts succeeded in placing it on the Statute Book. But it represented no triumph for him. It sparked off endless trouble for him both at home and abroad. The Indians rejected the Act completely; they refused to accept the communal franchise as adequate compensation for the loss of their rights. They named it the 'Ghetto Act' and started a campaign of passive resistance against it. The Indian Congress appealed to the Indian Government for support, and inevitably India was involved in the matter.

Throughout the debate on the Bill, there was a reluctance to face up to the international implications of the Indian question. Speakers on all sides of the House insisted that the Indian question was entirely a domestic matter to be settled by the Parliament of South Africa. They denounced the Indian Congress for invoking the aid of India, a course which, they contended, was a challenge to the Government of South Africa and a denial of its sovereignty. The Indians by appealing to an outside Power were doing their cause no good and were forfeiting their claim to citizenship.

This theme ran through most of the speeches, but the very force and frequency with which it was repeated constituted a recognition of the fact that the issue had already gone beyond the scope of a domestic dispute. India made it clear that she would not renounce her concern for the fate of the Indian minority in South Africa until their rights and dignities were placed on an acceptable and assured basis. India recalled the Indian High Commissioner, broke off diplomatic and trade relations with South Africa and on 22 June made application to the United Nations to place 'the treatment of Indians in South Africa' on the agenda of the General Assembly. Thus, whether Smuts liked it or not, India lifted the whole issue out of the domestic sphere on to the international plane as a matter of dispute between South Africa and India. South Africa's racial policies had brought it at last into open conflict with an outside power and that power a fellow-member of the Commonwealth.

It was a particularly unhappy situation for Smuts. He, the staunch champion of the Commonwealth, was now responsible for the first serious rift in the structure which he had always defended and lauded, on holistic grounds, as a force making for peace and stability. Smuts could not have been taken unawares. As far back as 1923, Sir Tej Bahadur Sapru, the Indian delegate to the Imperial Conference, addressing himself to Smuts, said 'I tell him frankly that if the Indian problem in South Africa is allowed to fester much longer it will pass beyond the bounds of a domestic issue and will become a question of foreign policy of such gravity that upon it the unity of the Empire may founder irretrievably.' [8] It was a warning to Smuts that South Africa could enjoy immunity for her domestic policies only as long as Britain maintained its imperial rule over India; but the moment India attained its independence and gained control over its foreign policy, it would insist on a new dispensation for the Indian minority in South Africa. Now the day of reckoning had come. And here was the author of the Preamble to the United Nations Charter the first to be arraigned before that august assembly for violating its principles.

Smuts attended the United Nations in person. The purpose of his mission was to win the approval of the United Nations for his plan to incorporate South West Africa in the Union. When he got there, however, he found that his main task was to defend his Government against the onslaught of the Indian delegation on the question of the treatment of the Indian minority in South Africa. He had also to face the hostility of India on the question of South West Africa. Mrs Pandit, the head of the Indian delegation, led the attack against Smuts on both issues. She was a most formidable adversary; in six lengthy speeches, several of them lasting two or three hours, she kept up a sustained and relentless attack both in the General Assembly and in the Committees to which the issues were referred. She not only captured the sympathy of the General Assembly but swept it along on a wave of indignation against South Africa.

Mrs Pandit argued that the Asiatic Land Tenure and Indian Representation Bill fell within the jurisdiction of the United Nations because (1) it repudiated the Cape Town Agreement of 1927[1] which had pledged the Union Government to uplift the Indian community, (2) it violated the Charter of the United Nations, and (3) it created a situation likely to impair friendly relations between India and South Africa.

In reply Smuts contended that the Cape Town agreement had created no treaty obligations, and therefore South Africa was not guilty of breaking any treaty with India. His main contention, however, was that the Asiatic Land Tenure and Indian Representation Act was a matter which fell essentially within the domestic jurisdiction of South Africa. He argued that if peace were to be preserved in the world it was essential to uphold Article 2 (7) of the Charter, which was specifically designed to ensure that there would be no encroachment on the domestic jurisdiction of any State. 'Smuts', says Hancock, 'was pinning his whole case on a legal argument. It got him nowhere.' [9]

That it got him nowhere is not surprising. Smuts, as one of the architects of the United Nations, must have known that his was a barren defence, quite out of keeping with the spirit of the new world-order the United Nations Charter sought to establish. In terms of the rules which had hitherto governed diplomatic practice and the relations between nations, a purely legal argument might be cogent and effective. But it was precisely because of the disastrous inadequacy of these rules that the United Nations had been brought into being, and its authority defined in a Charter designed to supersede ancient diplomatic practices, which, in general, ensured that the will of the stronger would prevail. Could South Africa as a member-state which had subscribed to the principles of the United Nations Charter plead that the Indian question was a domestic matter and that to invoke the United Nations was in fact a trespass on her sovereignty? Had the United Nations no right to concern itself with the fate of the Indian minority in South Africa, even though their fate was the subject matter of a dispute between India and South Africa? Must a respect for national sovereignty take precedence in all circumstances over the need to keep the peace between nations?

The United Nations is not only concerned with stopping an act of aggression, either actual or impending. It is much more concerned with eliminating the fundamental causes of war. Many of the root-causes of war, such as religious persecution, racial discrimination, oppression of minorities, lie within the domestic sphere. The grievances of minorities are notoriously among the most potent of war-breeding phenomena. The Sudeten problem which led to the dispute between Germany and Czechoslovakia is a classical example. The Indian problem in South Africa is similar. It brought South Africa into conflict with India, a conflict which lifted the issue out of the domestic sphere on to the international plane, and on that level the United Nations was obliged to deal with it. It would, in fact, be impossible for the United Nations to perform its function of maintaining international order if it had no power to intervene in matters which, having their origin in the domestic sphere, emerge as subjects of dispute between nations.

Basically Smuts had a weak case; and he went on to use an argument which seems to indicate that he was conscious of the inadequacy of his case. In reply to Mrs Pandit's charge that South Africa's racial policies were indefensible Smuts said that by the same token India's caste-system was equally reprehensible. In using the *tu quoque* argument Smuts set an unfortunate precedent. It is an argument still used by South Africa's representatives at the United Nations to justify her racial policies, and because it bears the imprimatur of Smuts it is supposed to have some special merit. There is, in fact, no efficacy in the plea that South Africa is not the only country that practises racial discrimination; nor can South Africa derive any comfort from the argument that her accusers at the United Nations do not come with clean hands. The fact remains that, in the civilised world, South Africa is the only country that enshrines racial discrimination in her Statute Book and gives it the force of law. Whilst the other countries are in process of legislating racial discrimination out of existence, South Africa is busy legislating racial discrimination into existence. It is this difference in direction which is creating a widening gap between South Africa and the rest of the civilised world. In a word, South Africa is marching firmly against the whole trend of human progress. In seeking to preserve South Africa as the last stronghold of White supremacy, the Government is condemning her to a dangerous isolation. This is a situation which cannot endure. Sooner or later, South Africa will have to put herself on the side of progress by renouncing racial discrimination. Only a fundamental change in her racial policies can restore South Africa to a dignified place in the society of civilised nations.

Smuts's mission to the United Nations ended in failure. He failed to vindicate South Africa against the damaging attack by India and he failed to establish his claim to the incorporation of South West Africa in the Union. The General Assembly passed by the required two-thirds majority a resolution stating that the treatment of Indians in the Union must be brought into conformity with the agreements concluded between the two Governments and the relevant provisions of the Charter. And by thirty-seven votes to none, with nine abstentions, the General Assembly adopted a resolution rejecting the incorporation of South West Africa into the Union and it requested the Union Government to administer the territory 'in the spirit of the principles laid down in the Mandate'.

The result could not be otherwise. Even at that early stage the United Nations was a predominantly non-White organisation, reflecting the redistribution of political influence in the post-war world. Of the fifty-one original members of the United Nations, no less than twenty-seven were ex-colonial countries. The fact that the United Nations was predominantly non-White enhanced its significance. If the United

Nations meant anything at all, it meant that the non-White races had achieved a status of equality and that the epoch of White supremacy was over. The newly emancipated powers, who constituted the African-Asian group, could no longer be treated as a negligible factor in world affairs. They proclaimed in unmistakable terms that they were not prepared to accept a position of inferiority merely because of colour. They were determined to champion the cause of those non-White races who had not yet achieved their emancipation. Moreover, in their fight for the liberation of those non-White races who were still subject to discrimination or oppression they could count on the support of the Latin American states and important Western powers, notably the United States.

Thus, at the United Nations, Smuts faced a new world. It was a world he had helped to create, but he now faced it as a transgressor, arraigned for violating the principles which he himself, with a dedicated hand, had written into the preamble of the Charter. The spotlight of world opinion played steadily and fiercely on the proceedings, probably all the more so because Smuts in person was involved. It was a bitter experience for Smuts, and indeed a new experience, for it was the first time in his career that he had emerged from a high international assembly with his stature sadly diminished and the prestige of his country sadly damaged.

'The world', he wrote, 'does not know or understand us and we feel this deeply, even when we are conscious that we are much to blame for it all. It is a good country and a good people, but the world sees its mistakes more clearly than its goodness and virtues.

'I don't despair of the future, but it will not be easy to keep South Africa steady in this avalanche of condemnation which has so suddenly and unexpectedly overwhelmed it.' [10]

Hitherto Smuts had upheld the honour of South Africa with distinction; his prestige had served to enhance its status. In thinking well of Smuts the world invariably thought well of South Africa – his fame shed lustre upon his country. But now his prestige had declined: his power over assemblies had dwindled: there were no standing ovations to do homage to the prophet of a new world-order, to the great Commonwealth statesman who stood in the van of progress, to the great warrior who during the darkest days of the war had proclaimed, in ringing tones, his faith in the ultimate triumph of the 'Man of Nazareth' over the 'Man of Berchtesgaden'. At the United Nations, Mrs Pandit had 'cut him down to size'. He could fulfil no higher mission than to serve as the spokesman for a White ruling caste which, in a changing world, still insisted that it had an inherent right to a privileged status.

'I am suspected of being a hypocrite', he wrote, 'because I can be quoted on both sides. The Preamble of the Charter is my own work, and I also mean to protect the European position in a world which is tending the other way.'

But it was not only against the outside world that he had to defend his standpoint. At home, they also blamed him for the 'avalanche of condemnation' which had descended on South Africa.

'The Opposition', he wrote, 'naturally rejoices and puts all this to my account and to the liberalism (!) with which I have led the world astray. Here is the author of the great Preamble of the Charter exposed as a hypocrite and a double-faced time-server! They are of course all right . . . but look at this bad fellow who is responsible for it all.' [11]

This self-flagellation reveals something of the private agony he must have endured during and after his ordeal at the United Nations.

IV

Smuts returned home from his unhappy visit to the United Nations to face another challenge to his statesmanship. During his absence a crisis had arisen in the affairs of the Native Representative Council.

The Native Representative Council is now a forgotten institution. Its brief history is a forgotten episode. But its history, from its inception to its dissolution, remains a tragedy. As an institution it could have played a vital role in establishing a co-operative relationship between the regime and the Native peoples, between government and governed, and, in the fullness of time, it could, by its successful functioning, have given an immense impetus to the evolution of a common society in South Africa. Its fate, however, did not partake of the inevitability of a Greek tragedy; it owed its demise to the ineptitude of the Government. Indeed, nothing can bring home more poignantly the deficiencies of Smuts's pragmatic approach to the Native problem – a problem which in the post-war epoch should have been treated as a matter of paramount importance – than his unskilful handling of the Native Representative Council. The history of the Council constitutes a formidable indictment of the Smuts regime.

Smuts owed the N.R.C. more than a perfunctory interest – he was committed to it. The Council was an essential part of the *quid pro quo* for the removal of the Cape Natives from the common roll; it was therefore something more than a political make-weight in the legislative scales of 1936; and Smuts's acceptance of the bargain, which made it possible for Hertzog to place his Bill on the Statute Book, entailed upon him the obligation to make the Council work.

'The new Council', he said in 1936, 'would give the Natives a constitutional organ which they could use to express their grievances and declare their interests. He even looked forward to the day when the Council might become not merely the crown of local self-government for the Native community but a legislative body on a national scale.'

The Council was from the first an impressive body. Prominent among its members were: Dr John Dube, the head and founder of a large school in Natal, and the first president of the African National Congress – the University of South Africa conferred upon him the honorary degree of Doctor of Philosophy, the first Native to receive such an honour; Selope Thema, the first editor of the *Bantu World*, a powerful speaker and remarkable for a clear, logical and incisive mind; Mack Jabavu and R. H. Godlo, both journalists, the former an editor of an important paper. Professor Z. K. Matthews, professor of Law and Native Administration at the University College of Fort Hare, and Mr Paul Mosaka, a fiery and eloquent speaker, considered the most brilliant student Fort Hare had ever had, were elected to the Council in 1943. And Chief Albert Luthuli, the future winner of the Nobel peace prize, joined the Council in 1948. These were probably the most outstanding of the Councillors whose general level of attainment in various fields was very high. It was not surprising, however, that the Native Community could produce representatives of such high calibre; for the South African Natives had been in contact with Western civilisation far longer than any other Black community in Africa; they were therefore far more advanced, they had a deeper appreciation of Western values and a greater passion for advancement in civilised practices. Contact with Western civilisation had kindled aspirations which the backward tribal life could no longer satisfy, and they still held to the belief that the White man, who enjoyed such a rich heritage, would not begrudge them a share of it.

The debating skill of the Councillors was remarkable; moderation was the key-note of their discussions; and their wisdom and eloquence would have graced the proceedings of the highest forum in the land. It was most unfortunate that their debates did not receive the prominence they deserved. If the Government had adopted an imaginative approach to the work of the Council and, by appropriate techniques, had focussed attention on its activities, the Council would undoubtedly have gained the public esteem which it merited. Given an opportunity to function effectively, the Council would in time have convinced the White electorate that a community that could throw up leaders of such distinction could not be kept in a state of tutelage for ever, but deserved to participate in an electoral system which would promote their spokesmen to Parliament itself. If Smuts were genuinely anxious that the Council should achieve the goals he had held out to them, he would have co-operated with the Council to the full; he would have instilled in the Natives the conviction that the Native Representative Council was not part of a scheme to ensure permanent White supremacy, but was an important stage in the constitutional progress of the Native community – that, in a word, the Council was a half-way house and not a terminus.

The Native Councillors were not lacking in goodwill; they were ready to co-operate. They could not accept the Council as an adequate substitute for Parliamentary representation and a direct share in the making of the laws that governed them. But their main concern was the advancement of their people. By making a genuine effort to co-operate with their White rulers they hoped to achieve substantial gains for their people even within the narrow confines of the policy of segregation. They were ready to submit to a system of tutelage provided it was clearly understood that the Council was but a stage in their progress to full citizenship and direct participation in government.

Because of the co-operative attitude of the Native Councillors the first session began auspiciously. Hopes ran high.

'There is little doubt', says Mrs Ballinger[2], 'that the mere opportunity to state their side of the case on levels they had never reached before relaxed tension in people who had for so long been not politically inarticulate, but articulate beyond the range of government attention, and the Council terminated its first session in the hopeful and firm belief that it had come into being, as one member expressed it, as a third chamber of the legislature not only to be heard but to be listened to. Here indeed were grounds for encouragement and hope.' [12]

But the euphoria did not last much beyond the first session. As an advisory body the success of the Council depended entirely upon the degree of importance the Government was prepared to accord it: 'not only to be heard but to be listened to' meant in practice that its advice would not only influence but would be seen to influence legislation. But almost from the beginning it semed that the Government was anxious to avoid too close an association with the Council. It kept the Council always at arm's length lest the public might gain the impression that it, the Council, was actually exerting some influence on the course of legislation affecting Native interests. The Government, in short, took scarcely more than a perfunctory interest in the proceedings of the Council, treating it with the same lack of enthusiasm as the affluent acknowledge the claims of a poor relation.

Despite the earnest petitions of the Council, the Government made no effort to give it a home of its own, a dignified building which would establish its physical identity and enhance its status. Its proceedings, instead of being suitably publicised in the form of a printed Hansard, were recorded on roneoed sheets for limited circulation to those whom it may concern. The Minister of Native Affairs attended only the opening session to deliver a homily which followed a stereotyped pattern, claiming some kudos for what the Government had done for the Natives and warning the Council not to make demands which the Government would deem excessive and White public opinion would not countenance. The Secretary of Native Affairs, a civil servant, was Chairman designate of the Council, which meant that matters of policy could not be raised or, if raised, would receive no official recognition, and that the Councillors must confine their attention to matters of administration and the detail of legislation.

Very soon it became apparent to the Council that it was making no visible impact on the legislative process. It lost confidence in the efficacy of its role as an advisory body: so far from being a 'third legislature' it could discover no useful function for itself within the existing constitutional framework of the Union. The business of advising the Government and preparing draft legislation remained the function of the Ministerial departments and the Native Affairs Commission, a body consisting exclusively of Whites, nominated by the Government.

The Native Representative Council came to the conclusion that they must demand certain changes if they were to continue to function. They requested that the Minister of Native Affairs be present at all future meetings of the Council, and that the other Ministers be present when the Council had occasion to deal with their respective departments. They decided also that, firstly, the Council's own members must be increased and that it must be given certain legislative powers, and, secondly, that the Native Representation in Parliament must be increased. The Council appointed a 'Recess Committee on Representation' to consider and report on these proposals. In due course the Recess Committee made *inter alia* the following recommendations:

1. That if European representation in the Senate is at any time increased, Native representation should likewise be proportionately increased.
2. That the Native Representation in the House of Assembly be increased from 3 to 10 members.
3. That the number of elected members in the Native Representative Council be increased from 12 to 48.
4. That the Council be granted legislative powers, the Government to decide the nature and extent of such powers. [13]

It is difficult to understand why Smuts did not accept some, if not all, of these recommendations. They were by no means revolutionary. In fact, they were well within the framework of the segregation policy and were perfectly consistent with the system of communal representation established by the 1936 legislation. The Act of 1936 actually made provision for the enlargement of the membership of the Native Representative Council. General Hertzog himself had intended originally to assign legislative powers to the Council. The proposal to increase the Parliamentary representation from three to ten members may seem excessive; but in view of the fact that Hertzog's original measure, the draft Bill of 1926, made provision for seven Native Representatives, a request for three more than the original number, making a total of ten, cannot be considered exorbitant, especially after a lapse of eighteen years.

Smuts's acceptance of these proposals would have restored the confidence of the Council in the Government's good intentions and immensely improved race relations without jeopardising in any degree the policy of segregation. And one proposal at least would have been in his own interests – it would have strengthened his position politically. A Bill to increase the Native Representation in Parliament to ten would not have met with more resistance than he had to contend with in the matter of the Indian Land Tenure and Representation Act, a measure which, despite the fact that it aroused intense antagonism, some of it within his own party, he succeeded, largely by exerting his great personal authority, in carrying to the Statute Book. Indeed, there was a certain irony in his treatment of the Indians as compared with his treatment of the Natives. The Indians were given communal representation but refused it because it was a segregation measure; the Natives wanted seven more representatives but were refused them, despite the fact that their demand fell within the segregation policy. Smuts would satisfy neither the Indians nor the Natives. It was particularly unfortunate that Smuts would not accede to the request for an increase in the Native representation in Parliament. Seven more Native Representatives in Parliament would have saved him from disaster after the crucial election of 1948; for the Native Representatives would have been pro-Smuts and their support would have made it unnecessary for him to surrender power to Malan.

Why then did Smuts not accept at least some of the Council's proposals? Why did he not go some way towards meeting the demands of the Councillors and offer them some concession which, as an earnest of the Government's intentions, they would have appreciated much beyond its intrinsic worth? One searches in vain for an adequate explanation. Part of the explanation – a goodly part – lay in the personal make-up of Smuts himself. Smuts's character was highly complex; he was a living web of contradictions. Unlike most politicians, he had more than one persona; and of his several personae, it would be hard to say which one represented the true Smuts in a greater degree than any of the others. The inner core, the conative centre of his being, was impenetrable. On the one hand, he was depicted as a man of iron will, forceful and dynamic in the field of action. On the other hand, as Hofmeyr, who worked with him closely, observed, he was possessed of a peculiar inertia – a dilatoriness; he was prone to 'let things develop'. In debate, the Opposition used this phrase as a frequent taunt against Smuts, but of course they gave it a sinister interpretation, suggesting that he deliberately held his hand until the situation called for ruthless action.

This man, Smuts, who could be high-handed and imperious in the administrative sphere, was strangely cautious and even timid in taking a political initiative. He ruled his Cabinet with a rod of iron; no one, save Hofmeyr, dared to question his decisions – disagreement would have been a sign of insurrection. Yet in the House his style was placatory – he never struck an angry or aggressive note. He preferred the minor key even when debating great issues. He would rather propitiate the Opposition by conceding an element of validity in their case than triumph over them by a display of superior debating skill, of which he was eminently capable. His handling of the Indian question was typical of his pragmatic approach. He took action because the situation, mounting to a crisis, forced his hand. He was faced in Natal by a revolt against the United Party and the likelihood of a wholesale defection to the Dominion Party; he sought to allay the agitation by perpetuating the iniquitous Pegging Act and at the same time he tried to sugar-coat the pill for the Indians by offering them a communal franchise (which, unfortunately for Smuts, they rejected as being too meagre to compensate them for the loss of their rights). Where the Native Representative Council was concerned, he was faced with a different situation; he was under no compulsion to act. In the case of Natal, agitation had led to action. But in the case of the Council, action would lead to agitation. Smuts knew that any concession to the Natives would be supported without any enthusiasm and probably with great reluctance by his own followers, and that it would undoubtedly provoke a storm of protest from the Opposition. Why then stir up trouble when there was no imperative call for action? Smuts, therefore, obeyed his natural inclination and made no attempt, by timely concession, to allay the mounting discontent of the Native Councillors.

So Smuts let an opportunity for a great act of statesmanship go by. The Native Councillors became more resentful as they continued to work under the same unchanging conditions. Their mood darkened. They saw that within the framework of the segregation policy there was no scope for even the most limited reforms. As long as they had no real share in political power they could expect very little at the hands of their White rulers. Even Smuts, at the very height of his power, would not use his immense authority to ensure their advancement. The prospects he had held out to them in such eloquent terms at the inauguration of the Native Representative Council were illusory. Even the modest goals he had defined at the time were beyond their reach; and he had now served notice on them that those goals were even beyond their aspirations. Clearly then the policy of segregation, by depriving them of any share in political power, deprived them of any prospect of advancement.

They had undoubtedly received benefits from the Smuts Government. Hofmeyr, in two successive budgets, had extended old-age pensions and invalidity grants to the Natives. In 1945 a special Act made Native education a charge upon the Consolidated Revenue Fund; expenditure on Native education increased from £909,340 in 1939 to over £5,000,000 in 1947, and a substantial sum was earmarked for a school feeding scheme. In the fields of health and housing, the Government made increasing sums available to the local authorities. In the matter of wage-determination, the cost-of-living allowance was made obligatory. The Natives were ready to acknowledge that these benefits were substantial. But a Government even less benevolent in its paternalism would have had to confer these benefits on a poverty-stricken community whose labour was essential for the comfort and prosperity of their White masters. These benefits were dictated by the needs of an industrial society. The Government could not afford to carry the Native population as a heavy load of ineffectives. Their labour was indispensable, and if they were to make an effective contribution to the industrial development they could not be denied basic services in the field of housing, health and education, and at least sufficient wages to keep them alive and fit for work.

These benefits would have accrued to them even if there had been no Native Representative Council. The members of the Council were fully conscious of their role; they were not there to cup their hands in gratitude to their White benefactors – although they were always ready to make courteous acknowledgment for the benefits they received. They were not there to beg as a favour what their White rulers would, in their own interests, have to concede. Their function as Councillors was to exercise the rights of citizenship; they were there to take part in the legislative process, even if, at this stage, they could serve only in an advisory capacity. They were prepared to submit to a system of tutelage, although they considered themselves ready for emancipation, provided it was clearly recognised that it was but a stage in their progress towards full citizenship.

But they now discovered to their dismay that this prospect was closed to them. Clearly within the framework of segregation, which denied them any share in political power, there was no scope for advancement. They learnt that segregation, which in theory meant separate areas of freedom and development for White and Black, was in practice designed to keep them in a state of permanent subjection. Segregation, in short, was no more than a device to perpetuate White domination. As long as the Native Representative Council was prepared to accept an acquiescent role in the structure of segregation it doomed itself to impotence. The Councillors decided that their situation called for an entirely new strategy. To pursue objectives within the framework of segregation was a waste of time and a fruitless expenditure of effort. The policy of segregation, the source of all their disabilities, must be the object of their attack. They planned their campaign accordingly.

V

The new strategy was put into operation in the session of 1945. The opening address of the Minister of Native Affairs gave the Councillors their first opportunity of going into attack.

The war had come to an end, and the Minister had much to say in praise of the contribution of the Native people to the war effort:

'Out of the War has come a desire for a better social order and great sympathy for the aspirations of the Native people.

'The war effort of the Native people, especially the gallantry in the field that has resulted in many awards of bravery, has undoubtedly made a deep impression upon the national mind . . . a movement has been started among our European soldiers up North to establish a war memorial fund with the main purpose of providing better health services for the Native people . . . some £10,000 has already been voluntarily subscribed by each European soldier giving two days' pay.' [14]

The rest of the speech, following the usual pattern, drew attention to the increased amount of money which the Government had made available for Native welfare, especially to alleviate the effects of drought conditions in the Reserves, and to the Government's intention of proceeding with its plans for the rehabilitation of the Reserves. He ended up by making the usual appeal to the Councillors to conduct their deliberations with wisdom and moderation. Councillor Mosaka, in moving the customary vote of thanks to the Minister, said:

'It is not often that we have a Minister with us on our deliberations and when opportunity offers as it does now, we are all very keen to say a few words which ordinarily we would like to say, and we sometimes do say, but we always have the feeling that we never reach the right quarters. It is one of the purposes of this Council to advise the Government, but I always feel that we are advising the administrative officials who have been charged with carrying out a policy for which they themselves are not responsible.'

He then went on:

'Now, Sir, you have referred to the cessation of hostilities and the great wave of enthusiasm that has swept through the country, and the fact that everyone is looking forward to better days . . . I think that the time has come for a revision of the whole Native policy of this country . . . We think that the new spirit which is partially symbolised in the National War Memorial could find a greater and better expression in a change of Native policy, so that the Native can become an integral part of the life of South Africa.'

Councillor Mosaka's speech began the proceedings on a subdued but ominous note. It was when the Councillors opened up on the subject of the Pass Laws that the attack on the Government developed its full force. The debate was significant not because of the nature of the subject – the Pass Laws were under constant criticism – but because it was conducted in far more fiery terms than any previous debate, clearly reflecting the new mood of the Councillors. Councillor Mosaka said that, 'since the outbreak of the War the African people, by common consent, have decided that the Pass system was their Enemy No 1.

'The point of disappointment to me was that at the opening of this Council the Minister made no reference whatsoever to the Pass system. We had expected something big, something spectacular. We had expected a statement from the Minister to this effect – "You people have fought for peace and freedom and as a gesture of the new era which has set in we have now decided to abolish all passes and do away with the system!" Well instead of that the Government goes in the diametrically opposite direction. Instead of abolishing the Pass Laws, it says "we are going to extend the Pass system".'

Councillor Mosaka then went on to express his dismay at the fact that the Government had decided to transfer the control of passes from the Native Affairs Department to local authorities 'just at a time when we are asking for the abolition of those passes.

'You know the semblance of democratic rights which seems to be afforded to the Native people . . . by giving them representation in the Senate and in Parliament, and even through this bogus Council . . . that semblance of democratic rights is entirely wanting in local authorities. And yet the Government continually frames laws giving greater and greater authority to the Local Authorities, and no semblance of representation to the Native people under their care. And when you deny those people any representation in the City Council you deny the most articulate, the most advanced section of the Africans, the people who are in the Urban areas, any representation, and I say that the amount of tyranny you allow in the Local Councils does not justify your transferring what is already an oppressive measure to bodies which are only too ready to apply oppression even without their having the powers you now want to give to them.'

Councillor Thema said:

'This is a matter which touches my heart and makes my blood boil . . . We did hope that after this war the one thing the Government of this country would do would be to abolish the Pass Laws. Our Government however has turned a deaf ear to our requests . . . The time is coming when we shall have to preach Africa for the Africans . . . It will come if the White people persist in the attitude they are adopting.'

He concluded with a thrust at Smuts:

'As a statesman of world fame he has spoken of peace. Well, we want him to create peace in South Africa, the country in which he lives.'

This marked the end of co-operation and the beginning of confrontation.

VI

It was, however, in the session of 1946 that the new strategy precipitated the crisis which brought to an end the working relationship between the Government and the Council.

The session began in the most unpropitious circumstances. Two days before the Council met in Pretoria 50,000 Native mine workers went on strike; they demanded an increased pay of 10 shillings per shift. To back their demands a group of strikers marched on the Johannesburg City Hall. The police however fired on the marchers and drove them back, killing four of the strikers. At West Springs, on the very day the Council was meeting in Pretoria, 4,000 miners armed with iron bars and axes, so it was said, marched towards Johannesburg. Police, brought from all over the Witwatersrand, intercepted the marchers and using firearms drove them back, killing several of their number.

Smuts, addressing the head-committee of the United Party immediately before his departure for England, sought to justify the action of the police; the strikers, he said, had no real grievances – the strike was the work of agitators. Smuts, of all people, should have known that the agitator may thrive on discontent but he cannot create it. The agitator can be effective only when a state of unrest has already reached the point of crisis. It is always easier to blame the agitator than to deal with the causes of discontent. Smuts would have inspired more confidence in his handling of the situation if he had promised the mine-workers that he would institute an inquiry into their grievances.

It was therefore in a tense atmosphere that the Council met for its annual session. The news of the events on the Witwatersrand cast a gloom over the proceedings from the very outset. If that were not enough to disturb the equanimity of the Council, its members were immediately subjected to an unpardonable personal humiliation. Having no home or meeting-place of their own – for which they had unsuccessfully petitioned since 1938 – the Councillors were usually accommodated reasonably well, with suitable conveniences, in the Pretoria City Hall. But on this occasion the Pretoria City Council, dominated by a Nationalist majority, refused to give the necessary permission. The Councillors were herded into cramped quarters somewhere in the Department of Labour, where, apart from the absence of the usual facilities, they found that the lavatories were for Whites only.

This contemptuous treatment of the Council was, however, an appropriate if not an auspicious beginning to the session. Indeed, the herding of the Councillors into these cramped quarters was a master-stroke of planning – if its purpose was to heighten the feelings of frustration which the proceedings of the Council were destined to produce.

The members of the Council fully expected the Minister of Native Affairs to be present at the opening of the session, especially on this occasion, to make a statement on the grave situation in the mines. To their disappointment and dismay.

not only was the Minister absent, but the Chairman designate, the Secretary of Native Affairs, could not officiate as he had been called away because of the strike. A subordinate official took the chair. In his opening address, the Acting Chairman made no reference to the strike. Councillor Mosaka promptly asked for a statement, putting a series of questions on the strike situation. The Acting Chairman said it was very difficult to give an immediate statement; 'the whole position was so uncertain that it would be preferable to leave a statement to a later date when the position was clarified a little'. He said he would refer the questions to the Secretary for Native Affairs who would prepare a reply in due course. The Acting Chairman intimated that a Cabinet sub-committee was meeting at the moment on the subject of the strike. This immediately led to a heated debate. Councillor Mosaka made it clear that they could have no confidence in the findings of a Cabinet sub-committee. 'We hold the Government responsible for the shooting which has taken place, because, according to newspaper reports, the shooting took place on advice from Pretoria.' He went on:

'We would be more satisfied if our African representatives, the Representatives of the Africans in Parliament, were consulted in this matter; if members of this Council were also consulted about the negotiations which the Government is setting afoot. We do not think that justice can be done if a Cabinet sub-committee is merely going to meet by itself and is going to make decisions in regard to this whole matter. We want to be consulted on this question.' [15]

As the debate proceeded on these angry lines, Councillor Godlo announced that in view of the situation he could not give his attention to the agenda of the meeting and moved the adjournment in the following terms:

'We do not proceed with the items on the agenda until such time as we have been given a full statement in reply to those questions raised by Councillor Mosaka because those questions represent the voice of the Council as a body.'

The Acting Chairman, however, refused to allow the

motion and insisted that the Council should proceed with the ordinary business on the agenda. During the lunch-hour break, a caucus of the Council, in arranging the order of business for the rest of the day in accordance with established practice, decided to give precedence to the following motion by Councillor Moroka:

'This Council, having since its inception brought to the notice of the Government the reactionary character of the Union Native Policy of segregation in all its ramifications, deprecates the Government's post-war continuation of a policy of Fascism which is the antithesis and negation of the letter and spirit of the Atlantic Charter and the United Nations Charter. The Council, therefore, in protest against this breach of faith towards the African people in particular and the cause of world freedom in general, resolves to adjourn this session, and calls upon the Government forthwith to abolish all discriminatory legislation affecting non-Europeans in this country.'

The debate on this motion is memorable chiefly for the contribution of Councillor Mosaka whose speech was a bitter and scathing indictment of the Government in its dealings with the Council.

'The experiment has failed', he said, 'because the Government which is the author of segregation and therefore the author of the Native Representative Council never intended to honour its pledge – it has never bothered itself for one single moment about the Council. We have been fooled. We have been asked to co-operate with a toy telephone. We have been speaking into an apparatus which cannot transmit sound and at the end of which there is nobody to receive the message. Like children we have taken pleasure at the echo of our own voices.'

Councillor Thema also contributed a notable speech to the debate.

'This may be the beginning of the parting of the ways', he said, ominously, 'and I want to say that we on this side of the

Colour line have a clear conscience. We have tried our best to co-operate with the White people of this country, we have been loyal ever since the White man came to South Africa . . . White South Africa has turned a blind eye and a deaf ear to us here. They have failed to recognise the fact that Africans have been trying their level best to do the right thing and live at peace with them in this country.'

At the end of the debate the resolution moved by Councillor Moroka was carried unanimously. The Council then adjourned, the Councillors dispersed to their homes and now awaited the Government's response to the challenge.

Hofmeyr, who was acting Prime Minister in the absence of Smuts, had to cope with the situation. He realised that a turning-point had been reached in the Government's relations with the Council. He wrote to Smuts:

'It means that the hitherto moderate intellectuals of the Professor Matthews type are now committed to an extreme line against Colour discrimination and have carried the Chiefs with them. We can't afford to allow them to be swept into the extremist camp, but I don't see what we can do to satisfy them, which would be tolerated by European public opinion. The Native Representative Council was, however, a vital part of the 1936 legislation and if it cannot be made to function far-reaching questions will arise.' [16]

'Smuts replied', says Hancock, 'that the Government would have to liberalise its social policy, but it would have to carry public opinion along with it. Now that the war was over he had hopes of making rapid progress with a practical social policy away from politics.' [17]

Hofmeyr accepted this as a directive. After all he too was strongly in favour of a policy of social amelioration, and in the sphere of housing, health and education he had already done much for the Natives. He decided to make 'social policy away from politics' the theme of his reply to the Native Representative Council, which was due to reassemble on 20 November.

The Councillors looked forward with eager anticipation to

the meeting, especially as it was to be addressed by Hofmeyr. When the Council reassembled, their hopes ran high. Hofmeyr, whom the Africans had named Ntembu, meaning 'our hope', was the one man whose healing touch could mend the rift between the Government and the Council. In the gallery sat the members of the Native Affairs Commission and the Native Senators and Parliamentary Representatives; all were highly conscious of the importance of the occasion.

They were to receive a sharp disappointment. Hofmeyr began his speech on a note of rebuke; referring to the resolution of the Council, he said:

'I must commence by saying that we have noted with regret and surprise the violent and exaggerated statements which were made in support of the resolution – statements which were in many respects not in accord with the standards of responsibility to be expected from a body like this Council.' [18]

He then went on to deal with the resolution which demanded the abandonment forthwith of all discriminatory legislation affecting non-Europeans.

'It should be clear to the Council', he said, 'that it would not be practicable to accede to this request if account was to be taken not only of the process of adjustment that was taking place between the different peoples living in the Union, but also of the interests of the Native people themselves. Many of the differential provisions in the existing laws of which exception is taken were in fact enacted to protect Native interests, and if they were indiscriminately to be removed those interests could not but suffer.'

He cited, as an example of discriminatory legislation which protected Native interests, the Land Acts, in terms of which land owned or occupied by Natives was not open to purchase by other than Natives, thus securing them against predatory European competition.

He then went on to tell them, 'at the risk of repeating what has been said on other occasions', what the Government had done to improve the lot of the Natives, how expenditure on education had increased, how the health services had been improved, and how greater provision had been made for housing; he told them of the Government's scheme for training Native builders for Native areas and that the Government would take an early opportunity of introducing legislation to provide for the recognition of Native trade unions. The Government however did not propose to give recognition to a trade union for Native Mineworkers, for whom other channels of representation would be made available. And finally he drew attention to the further land purchases for Natives in terms of the 1936 legislation.

Hofmeyr ended his summary with the claim that all these benefits had been given freely and in many cases without any specific request from the Council. To tell the Councillors that Government benevolence rendered their services largely gratuitous was perhaps not the most tactful way to restore a co-operative relationship between the Government and the Council. Yet Hofmeyr was strictly logical. As the Government had decided to pursue a 'practical social policy away from politics', there was virtually no role for the Council – Government paternalism would do all that was required to improve the lot of the Native. But the Council was far more concerned about citizen status and political rights than about the social benefits that were due to them; they could not, therefore, accept Hofmeyr's claim that his account of the social benefits which had accrued to them 'as an earnest of the Government's general attitude of goodwill to the Native people, as a proof of its desire for their advancement' was an answer to the resolution passed by the Council.

This was immediately made clear to Hofmeyr by Chief Poto, who, in thanking the Acting Prime Minister for his presence – a customary act of courtesy – said:

'We know that you have various calls in different directions, but we feel we have as much claim on your presence in our midst from time to time as any other section of the community . . . We can foresee that the downfall of this Council can only be caused by the Government itself . . . by that

Government's failing to attach the significance to this Body which is due to it.'

And Councillor Thema, in seconding the vote of thanks, said more pointedly: 'We cannot live in South Africa as masters and servants, but we can live here as partners because this country belongs to you and it belongs to us.'

Clearly, Hofmeyr's speech was received with deep dismay. It was the sort of speech which Major v. d. Bijl could have made without discredit to himself. But coming from Hofmeyr, regarded as the greatest liberal of his time, the effect on the Councillors was shattering; it dealt a mordant blow to their hopes. The speech was also a bitter disappointment to Hofmeyr's friends and admirers who had gathered in the gallery to listen to him. The Government, it was abundantly clear, would not exceed the bounds of a benevolent paternalism; it was not prepared to delegate a measure of responsibility to the Council, and was even less disposed to sharing political power in any form.

Some five days later, Professor Matthews drew up a statement, unanimously supported by the Councillors, which represented the considered reply of the Council to Hofmeyr's speech.

'To us', the statement read, 'it seemed to be merely an apologia for the *status quo*, apparently oblivious of the progressive forces at work not only in the world in general but in South Africa itself. The statement makes no attempt to deal with the burning questions of the day, such as the Pass Laws, the colour bar in industry, the political rights of the non-Europeans in the Union, etc., and in effect it raises no hopes for the future as far as the African people are concerned . . . In his statement the Acting Prime Minister virtually denies that the Native policy of the Union is in need of revision and proceeds to justify the policy of segregation and discrimination on the grounds of its supposedly protective character.'

Professor Matthews moved 'that pending a more reassuring reply from the Government the proceedings of the Council be suspended'.

The Government's reply arrived promptly the next morning. The Chairman, immediately after prayers, read it to the members. 'The Government finds itself unable to vary its decision.' It ended on a placatory note. 'The Council has rendered a contribution of great value to the progress which has so far been made. It is most desirable that, in the interests of the Native people themselves, the Council should continue to play its part in the promotion of their further advancement . . .'

Professor Matthews thereupon moved the adjournment of the Council for a brief interval to enable the Councillors to study the Acting Prime Minister's reply. The Acting Chairman made an earnest appeal to the Councillors, urging them not to take any drastic step which would impair their relations with the Government. Professor Matthews said that the Councillors would consider the reply to see whether 'it makes possible the co-operation which you have asked for, and which we are very willing to give, provided we can give it on conditions of dignity and self-respect.'

When the Council reassembled at 2.30 p.m. Professor Matthews moved the following resolution:

'That this Council, having carefully considered the further reply of the Acting Prime Minister, finds itself unable to discover in his statement any disposition on the part of the Government to undertake a revision of its Native policy in order to bring it into line with the changing conditions of African life.

'Since its inception this Council has loyally co-operated with the Government and would continue to do so as long as it is not expected either expressly, or by implication, to sacrifice in the process the legitimate rights and interests of the African people.

'In the circumstances, this Council feels compelled to adjourn the session in order to make it possible for Councillors to make fully known to the African people the nature and contents of the Acting Prime Minister's statement.

'This Council makes a further appeal to the Government to undertake such revision of its Native policy with a view to making possible co-operation between White and Black in this country.'

Professor Matthews's resolution was passed unanimously and the Council adjourned. It was to prove the last meeting of the Council under the Smuts regime.

When Smuts returned from his mission to the United Nations he found the deadlock between the Government and the Council was complete. A serious situation had developed. The African National Congress which had held a crisis conference in Bloemfontein strongly backed the Councillors in their stand. The Congress did not oppose any further attempts on the part of the Councillors to meet the Government but decided that in future the African people must boycott the elections of both the Native Representative Council and the Native Representation in Parliament. Thus the A.N.C. rejected the system of separate representation.

On his return Smuts took immediate steps to break the deadlock. He decided to invite six members of the Council to meet him and to consider what might be done to restore a co-operative relationship between the Government and the Council.

'The Prime Minister himself,' says Mrs Ballinger, 'when he met the group he had selected, said he had no plan to offer, but he suggested the possibility of an enlarged Council under an African Chairman of the Council's own choosing and the addition to its consultative powers of a share in the special legislative and administrative power which they exercised in Native areas. He further suggested a closer link-up of the Council with the urban Townships through elected local boards and a strengthened and statutory national conference of such boards to speak authoritatively for the growing urban population . . . He made it clear that these suggestions were purely tentative, "a bone to chew on" he called it.' [19]

The bone, however, was too meagre. It offered no nourishment of the kind they sought. The Councillors did not hesitate to tell him so. When by November the Prime Minister had failed to meet the Council in accordance with a promise he had made to do so, the Councillors themselves met in conference and, as a result of their deliberations, they issued a statement in the following terms:

'Referring to the fact that the Prime Minister had not so far met the Council, they felt justified in attributing his reluctance in this regard to a desire on his part to await the election of a new Council, due early in 1948, in the hope that its members would be "more amenable to Government control and guidance" than those who had been responsible for the deadlock then existing between the Council and the Government.

'As for the proposals themselves, they appreciated that these were tentative in form and substance and might ultimately be drastically altered but their very tentative nature made any decision on the Council's part difficult. As they stood, they gave no guarantee of an intention on the part of the Government to go to the root of the trouble which had caused the deadlock, that was the need for a new approach to Native policy which would recognise the inter-dependence of Black and White, and open the door to citizenship to the African people . . .

'The proposals they declared were entirely consonant with the familiar policy of separation, a policy which engendered a spirit of hostility and racial bitterness between Black and White, as against that of mutual co-operation in the interests of both sections of the community. What was required, both to heal the breach between the Council and the Government and to restore the confidence of the Native people, was, they said, a policy that would give the Native people a sense of security; a policy which was flexible and could readily be adapted to changing conditions and varying circumstances; in fact, a policy which recognised that Natives were citizens of this country and not a thing apart.' [20]

The statement, though firm and uncompromising in tone and content, indicates very clearly that they were anxious to keep open a channel of communication with the Government. They clearly repudiated the policy of boycott by calling upon the Africans to return to the Council in the forthcoming

would return in triumph and once more light the way to progress. Despite the disillusionment they had experienced under Smuts, such a disaster as the defeat of the United Party was inconceivable. After all, the Nationalist Party, which drew its inspiration from the past, was an anachronism. It had survived from a previous epoch: its traditional outlook rendered it quite incapable of meeting the challenge of a dynamic and changing society. The narrow and exclusive nationalism it sought to revive had lost its purpose and *raison d'être* in a modern industrial society. The Nationalist Party could not survive defeat in the coming election; its day was over. A triumphant United Party would at least keep the road open to progress; it would pave the way for a realignment of political forces – party divisions would be determined not by racial divisions but by economic forces, as in every modern society. A victory for the United Party would be the beginning of a new era.

Those, however, who were confident of a United Party victory, underestimated the tenacity of the Nationalist Party, and their highly practised skill in reducing the political debate to a level where the appeal to fear and prejudice and not reason was the decisive factor. Malan, despite his massive stolidity and an owlish fixity of gaze which suggested sluggish cerebration, was an agile politician and an extremely shrewd strategist. With unerring instinct he decided upon a strategy which would ensure that the colour question would emerge as the dominant issue in the election. Firstly he made use of the element of surprise; he announced boldly that Republicanism – generally regarded as the Nationalist Party's most sacred tenet – would not be an issue in the election; it would be decided by a referendum when the time was ripe. He dropped anti-Semitism; he banished all talk of making Afrikaans the sole official language and reducing English to an inferior status. He promised that a Nationalist Government would be generous in its treatment of the returned soldiers. And finally he vindicated his claim to patriotism by declaring that the Nationalist Party would not be neutral in a war against Russia. After these preliminary manoeuvres Malan was ready for battle.

He made his position clear in a key-note address at Paarl on 20 April 1948. 'Will the European race', he asked, 'in the future be able to and also want to maintain its race, its purity and its civilisation or it will float along until it vanishes in the black sea of the South African non-European population.' [21] Smuts, he continued, was doing nothing to save South Africa from the rising tide of Colour. Smuts in fact was ready to open the flood-gates. Was he not grooming Hofmeyr as his successor? A Hofmeyr Government was not compatible with the survival of White South Africa. Thus Malan flung down the gage of battle. It was to be a *'swart gevaar'* election with a vengeance!

How did Smuts prepare to meet the challenge? In March 1948 the Fagan Commission issued its report. It found that the movement of the Natives to the urban industrial areas was a natural economic phenomenon engendered by necessity and would continue –, the movement could be guided and regulated but it was impossible to prevent it or turn it back. Territorial segregation was completely impracticable and migratory labour was an obsolete system. Henceforth the Natives must be accepted as a settled, permanent part of the urban population and the Government must plan its legislation accordingly. The Fagan report confirmed what Smuts had stated clearly and convincingly in his address to the Institute of Race Relations in 1942. Smuts, however, had been too cautious to initiate any changes in Native policy on the strength of his own analysis of the Native problem. He wanted an authoritative document like the Fagan report to prepare the public mind for reforms which he knew were necessary and even inevitable. Politically it may have been a prudent procedure to await the report. But unfortunately the report was issued almost on the eve of the election, far too late to serve the purpose he had in view.

However, the situation demanded of Smuts an immediate and clear statement of policy. Smuts presented himself as the exponent of the middle way. Speaking in the Johannesburg City Hall at a pre-election rally, he declared, 'The Nationalists do not want to see the middle way that South Africa has followed all these years.' What in practical terms did he mean by the 'middle way'? It meant, first of all, that he would stand firmly by the Native Representation established by the 1936 legislation. From that system of representation he would not retreat; but neither did he promise any advance on it. Socially and economically, he accepted the findings of the Fagan report, and he formally announced that the United Party accepted the principles and proposals recommended by the Fagan Commission – a declaration which meant very little to the average voter.

Whatever the merits of the Fagan report, it was highly unlikely that such a sophisticated document would have a decisive influence on the public mind immediately before a general election. Moreover, it was ingenuous to assume that in the atmosphere of the hustings the political debate could be kept on the objective level of the Fagan report. The Nationalists were adept at reducing the debate to the level where emotion and not reason would prevail; their aim was to ensure that fear and prejudice would be the decisive factor. Thus the influx of the Natives into the towns, which the Fagan report showed conclusively was the natural and inevitable response to the needs of a developing industrial society – whose progress was now completely dependent on Native labour – was condemned as a menace and treated as the most serious aspect of the *'swart gevaar'*. This influx was depicted in the most exaggerated terms as the equivalent of a barbarian invasion. And of course it was the United Party, and not the process of industrialisation, which had opened the gates to the savage hordes who were now pouring into the urban areas. What future was there for the White man under such a regime?

Malan, scornfully rejecting the Fagan report, offered his own solution – the policy of apartheid. It was the new panacea. Apartheid was in fact merely a new name for the old segregation policy which previous Governments had followed and had become a traditional policy. 'Apartheid', however, was used to differentiate it from the segregation policy on which the 1936 legislation was based and which Hertzog had offered as a final settlement of the Native problem – a settlement which Malan now opposed, demanding in particular the abolition of the Native Representation in Parliament and the abolition of the Native Representative Council. Moreover, apartheid was offered as a more thorough-going concept than segregation and was designed to operate on all fronts where the White and the non-White races might come into contact with each other. Apartheid became a slogan of remarkable potency; its impact was swift and immediate; it leapt into the newspaper headlines; it dominated every discussion on race relations; it seemed the magic formula by which a Nationalist Government would solve South Africa's most intractable problem; it exercised a mesmeric influence on the public mind.

But what precisely did apartheid mean? According to the Fagan report the integration of the Natives into the economic life of the country was an inevitable process. To offer the electorate a choice between apartheid and integration was to offer it a choice between a fantasy and a fact. The process of integration was irreversible – indeed any attempt to reverse the process of integration was as vain as an attempt to make the rivers flow back to their source.

To give a semblance of plausibility to their policy, the Nationalists took refuge in an elaborate piece of make-believe. In order to prove that apartheid was not a fantasy, they had to pretend that integration was not a fact. The Natives were only temporary sojourners in the White areas. They were there only for the convenience of their White employers. Their ultimate destination was some vague Utopia in the Reserves, their ethnic homelands. There they would enjoy all the rights and freedoms which, as aliens, they could not claim in the White areas. So eventually the Natives would fold their metaphorical tents and take themselves off to their mythical homes in their hypothetical Bantustans.

In actual fact the Natives in the so-called White areas had no more prospect of returning to their homelands than the descendants of the early White settlers had of returning to their countries of origin – to Holland, France or England. As the Fagan report stated authoritatively and clearly, these Natives had to be accepted as a permanent part of the urban population; they were permanently settled in the so-called White areas. Yet in terms of the Nationalist Party policy, they would have no say in the making of the laws which governed them and which they must obey; they would have no trade union rights, no power to bargain for their living standards; they would have no right to own and occupy homes in the areas where they were permanently settled. They would have no rights whatsoever. The promise of a bright future in the Reserves – which they would never see – was offered as a justification for depriving the Natives of even elementary rights in the so-called White areas. Clearly, apartheid was no more than a device to perpetuate White domination.

As in every election, there was a 'grievance vote'. During the dark days of the war, the people were prepared to put up with austerity measures – they put up with rationing, with shortages, with standing in queues. But with the return of peace, they felt that austerity was unnecessarily prolonged, and even the absence of white bread and mutton was treated as a grievance. So they regarded the election as an opportunity to register their displeasure with a Government at whose hands they suffered these privations.

One dominant note, however, rose above the tumult of the hustings – the appeal to colour prejudice. The question of a Republic had been removed from the political arena; but this did not mean that the Nationalists were to renounce the appeal to Afrikaner National sentiment. The call to the blood was too valuable a factor to be left unexploited. It would have to play its part in luring wayward Afrikaners back to the fold. It was used to reinforce the main election theme. Apartheid and Afrikaner Nationalism were not two distinctive concepts. They were two aspects of the same thing. Apartheid was designed to ensure White *Baasskap*.[3] White *baasskap* meant the supremacy of Nationalist Afrikanerdom. The Nationalist Party was therefore not only the true home of the Afrikaner but it was the only party that could safeguard his privileged status as a member of the White ruling caste. The United Party could offer nothing so robust as this Herrenvolk concept. The United Party stood for a broad South Africanism; how could such a party, which admitted even liberals to its ranks, offer salvation to the true Afrikaner striving to defend his heritage against the rising tide of Colour?

Malan in his election addresses insisted that the electorate were confronted with a fateful choice – apartheid or integration. He tried to dramatise the election as a clash of ideological opposites. The antithesis, however, was unreal. The Nationalist Party spoke of apartheid, and the United Party spoke of integration; but these terms did not define a difference – they disguised a fundamental identity. Both parties stood for White supremacy. The electorate were offered a choice between two versions of the same thing. They were asked to choose between White *Baasskap* which Malan promised to enforce and White supremacy which Smuts professed to uphold.

On the fateful day the electorate decided in favour of Dr Malan. He won the election by a majority of five seats over all other parties.

VIII

That, however, does not complete the story of this crucial election. An analysis of the voting reveals a startling but tragic fact. It shows conclusively that Smuts need never have lost the election.

It is the first business of a politician to take every legitimate step to ensure his return to power; in the struggle for power, a resolute politician will take no chances whatsoever. Smuts failed to take a necessary and legitimate precaution: despite the entreaties of his advisers, he had refused to alter the rules of delimitation which, in their existing form, conferred an undue advantage upon his opponents. He went into an election knowing that the dice were loaded against him.

For purposes of delimitation, the constitution drew a distinction between urban and rural constituencies. The number of voters constituting a rural seat could be reduced by as much as 15% below the standard quota; and on the other hand, the number of voters constituting an urban seat could be increased by as much as 15% above the standard quota. This meant that, at the extremes, 85 rural votes were equivalent in value to 115 urban votes. The effect of this 'load' and 'unload' as between urban and rural constituencies was to give an undue preponderance of seats to the rural areas where the strength of the Nationalist Party lay. This arrangement was decided upon at the time of Union and was designed to ensure that constituencies in the sparsely populated rural areas would not be too large, making it extremely difficult for Parliamentary representatives, with the means of transport available at the time, to keep in touch with their constituents. However, with the advent of modern transport and rapid communication there was no longer a justification for maintaining the 'load' and 'unload' as between town and country. Accordingly his advisers urged Smuts to alter the rules of delimitation. They argued very cogently that it was perfectly legitimate to do so; that the system was not entrenched and to change it required only a simple majority; and, above all, it was a just and fair proposal – for what could be more democratic than a system of delimitation based on the principle of one vote, one value? Smuts however would not hear of it. He cut his advisers short. 'The existing electoral arrangements,' he said, 'damaging to his own party though they were, had their roots in the pact of good faith which had created and must still sustain the Constitution.' [22] When a group of United Party M.P.s broached the subject with him he was less abrupt but equally obdurate in his refusal. He said he had complete confidence in his *platteland* following. 'I know my people,' he said. 'They are a good people. They will never let me down.'

Alas, the 'good people', whom he trusted so, let him down in his own constituency. In Standerton they rejected him in favour of an obscure young Nationalist, a newcomer to the political scene.

The election results were as follows:

Members Returned

For Malan – 79 members
For Smuts – 71 members

Thus Malan had a majority of eight over Smuts, but as the three Native Representatives supported Smuts, Malan's majority was reduced to five.

Votes

(Including estimates for uncontested seats)[4]

For Malan – a total of 462,332
For Smuts – a total of 588,518

As between Malan and Smuts the percentages were as follows:

For Malan – a total of 39.85%
For Smuts – a total of 50.72%

If each vote had the same value, the election would have produced the following result:

For Smuts – 80 seats
For Malan – 60 seats

On the basis of one vote one value, Smuts would have won the election by a majority of 20 seats over Malan. In addition there were 10 other members – one independent and nine belonging to other groups – and these of course would have supported Smuts as against Malan.

The Election figures tell the whole tragic story. South Africa's momentous election was decided by a minority vote. Smuts could have averted disaster if he had followed the advice which had been so strongly urged upon him.

'I take all the blame for what has happened,' said Smuts after the election. This beating of his breast was not mere ritual. The self-reproach was fully deserved. Politically, he had committed the unpardonable sin – power was within his grasp, but he let it slip through his fingers!

Malan could scarcely believe his good fortune. Power, like a gift from heaven, had fallen into his lap. Had the miracle really happened? He looked round the familiar landscape for reassurance; but everything, even the trees, looked different – they had a new look! And then suddenly he knew why! 'South Africa belongs to us again.' He issued a statement to this effect. 'Today South Africa belongs to us once more. For the first time since Union South Africa is our own and may God grant that it always remain our own.' Thus began the new era.

NOTES

[1] The Cape Town Agreement of 1927 made provision for an emigration scheme for those Indians who wished to return to India, and included a pledge by the South African Government to ensure the 'upliftment' of such Indians as might decide to remain in South Africa.

[2] Mrs Margaret Ballinger was one of the three Native Representatives elected to Parliament in 1937 and she held her seat until the Native Representation was abolished in 1959.

[3] Bossism: the Afrikaans equivalent for domination.

[4] In each uncontested seat, 6,500 votes were awarded to the winning party and 1,500 to the uncontesting party.

References

Section One

[1] S. G. Millin, *General Smuts*, Vol. I (Faber, 1936), p. 182.
[2] W. K. Hancock and Jean van der Poel (eds), *Selections from the Smuts Papers,* Vol. II (Cambridge University Press, 1966), p. 216.
[3] Quoted by Hancock, *Smuts*, Vol. I (Cambridge University Press, 1962), p. 215.
[4] Millin, *General Smuts*, Vol. I, p. 213.
[5] Quoted by G. H. Le May, *British Supremacy in South Africa* (Oxford University Press, 1965), p. 188.
[6] Hancock and van der Poel, *Selections from the Smuts Papers*, Vol. II, p. 238.
[7] Ibid., p. 242.
[8] Ibid., p. 450.
[9] Quoted by L. M. Thompson, *The Unification of South Africa* (Oxford University Press, 1960), p. 105.
[10] Millin, *General Smuts*, Vol. I, p. 251.
[11] Hancock and van der Poel, *Selections from the Smuts Papers*, Vol. II, p. 526.
[12] Ibid., p. 441.
[13] Ibid., p. 526.
[14] Ibid., p. 499.
[15] Walton, *The Inner History of the National Convention* (Maskew Miller, Cape Town, and Davis and Sons, Durban, 1912), p. 39.
[16] Ibid., p. 54.
[17] Ibid., p. 55.
[18] Ibid., p. 56.
[19] Ibid., p. 58.
[20] Ibid., p. 59.
[21] Ibid., p. 62.
[22] Ibid., p. 64.
[23] Ibid., p. 73.
[24] Ibid., p. 75.
[25] Ibid., p. 79.
[26] Ibid., p. 119.
[27] Ibid., p. 120.
[28] Ibid., p. 122.
[29] Ibid., p. 123.
[30] Ibid., p. 124.
[31] Ibid., p. 126.
[32] Ibid., p. 129.
[33] Ibid., p 130.
[34] Ibid., p. 133.

[35] Diary of F. S. Malan, p. 49.
[36] Walton, *Inner History of the National Convention*, p. 135.
[37] Ibid., p. 138.
[38] Diary of F. S. Malan, p. 57.
[39] Ibid., p. 59.
[40] Thompson, *Unification of South Africa*, p. 337.
[41] Diary of F. S. Malan, p. 247.
[42] Millin, *General Smuts*, Vol. I, p. 251.
[43] Thompson, *Unification of South Africa*, p. 232.
[44] Hancock, *Smuts*, Vol. I, p. 277.
[45] Hancock and van der Poel, *Selections from the Smuts Papers*, Vol. II, p. 441.
[46] Ibid., p. 561.
[47] Ibid., p. 546.
[48] *Hansard*, Vol. 64, 24 August 1948.
[49] Hancock, *Smuts*, Vol. I, p. 268.

Section Two

[1] Quoted by Hancock, *Smuts*, Vol. II (Cambridge University Press, 1968), p. 238.
[2] Ibid., p. 238.
[3] Quoted by Paton, *Hofmeyr* (Oxford University Press, 1964), p. 191.
[4] Ibid., p. 191.
[5] *Hansard*, 24 January 1933.
[6] Ibid., 1 February 1933.
[7] Jean van der Poel (ed.), *Selections from the Smuts Papers*, Vol. V (Cambridge University Press, 1973), p. 531.
[8] Ibid., p. 553.
[9] Hancock, *Smuts*, Vol. II, p. 252.
[10] Ibid., p. 254.
[11] Jean van der Poel (ed.), *Selections from the Smuts Papers*, Vol. VI (Cambridge University Press, 1973), p. 4.
[12] The Hofmeyr Papers, Library of the University of the Witwatersrand.
[13] *Hansard*, Joint Sitting, 27 January 1936.
[14] Ibid., 6 April 1936.
[15] Paton, *Hofmeyr*, p. 222.
[16] Hancock, *Smuts*, Vol. II, p. 275.
[17] Ibid., p. 276.
[18] Scott Haigh, *Strangers May Be Present* (Howard Timmins, Cape Town, 1951), p. 152.
[19] *Round Table* No. 117, December 1939, p. 204.
[20] Hancock, *Smuts*, Vol. II, p. 287.
[21] Ibid., p. 287.
[22] *Hansard*, Vol. 28, 1937.
[23] Paton, *Hofmeyr*, p. 263.
[24] Ibid., p. 262.
[25] van der Poel, *Selections from the Smuts Papers*, Vol. VI, p. 67.
[26] Hancock, *Smuts*, Vol. II, p. 292.
[27] Ibid., p. 292.

[28] L. Blackwell, *Farewell to Parliament* (Shuter and Shooter, Pietermaritzburg, 1946), p. 7.
[29] Ibid., p. 11.
[30] *Hansard*, Vol. 32, September 1938.
[31] Paton, *Hofmeyr*, p. 291.
[32] The Hofmeyr Papers.
[33] Hancock, *Smuts*, Vol. II, p. 457.
[34] Ibid., p. 298.
[35] Ibid., p. 308.
[36] Ibid., p. 309.
[37] *Sunday Times* (Johannesburg) 2 August 1964, p. 12.
[38] *Hansard*, 4 September 1939, Column 17 et seq.

Section Three

[1] *Hoernle Memorial Lecture*, 1942, S.A. Institute of Race Relations.
[2] *Hansard*, Vol. 52, 12 March 1945.
[3] Ibid., 14 March 1945.
[4] van der Poel (ed.), *Selections from the Smuts Papers*, Vol. VI, p. 425.
[5] Hancock, *Smuts*, Vol. II, p. 462.
[6] *Hansard*, Vol. 56, 25 March 1946.
[7] Ibid., 28 March 1946.
[8] Quoted by Hancock, *Smuts*, Vol. II, p. 139.
[9] Hancock, *Smuts*, Vol. II, p. 470.
[10] van der Poel (ed.), *Selections from the Smuts Papers*, Vol. VII, (Cambridge University Press, 1973), p. 116.
[11] Ibid., p. 117.
[12] M. Ballinger, *From Union to Apartheid*, (Bailey Bros, 1969), p. 155.
[13] Proceedings of the N.R.C. 1943, pp. 1-6.
[14] Ibid., Session November 1945, p. 2f.
[15] Ibid., Session August 1946.
[16] Quoted by Hancock, *Smuts*, Vol. II, p. 485.
[17] Ibid., p. 486.
[18] Proceedings of the N.R.C., Session November 1946, p. 2f.
[19] Ballinger, *From Union to Apartheid*, p. 198.
[20] Ibid., p. 199.
[21] Quoted by Hancock, *Smuts*, Vol. II, p. 500.
[22] Ibid., p. 506.

Index